MARJOE

MARJOE

THE LIFE OF MARJOE GORTNER

STEVEN S. GAINES

HARPER & ROW, PUBLISHERS
New York, Evanston, San Francisco, London

The author would like to thank the following people for their assistance: Barbara and Leonard Keilson, Laura and Buddy Bienenfeld, Lamour Sherwood, Rose and Harry Goshin, Ruth and Hal Gaines, Wayne Myers, and, of course, Phyllis Weintraub.

Photograph on title page by Joel Baldwin, *Life Magazine,* © Time, Inc. Photo on endpapers © Time, Inc.

MARJOE. Copyright © 1973 by Marjoe Gortner and Steven S. Gaines. All rights reserved. Printed in the United States of America. No part of this book may be used or reproduced in any manner whatsoever without written permission except in the case of brief quotations embodied in critical articles and reviews. For information address Harper & Row, Publishers, Inc., 10 East 53rd Street, New York, N.Y. 10022. Published simultaneously in Canada by Fitzhenry & Whiteside Limited, Toronto.

FIRST EDITION

STANDARD BOOK NUMBER: 06-011401-0

LIBRARY OF CONGRESS CATALOG CARD NUMBER: 72-9118

Designed by Gloria Adelson

HIS FIRST PUBLIC APPEARANCE

FOUR GENERATIONS
OF ORDAINED MINISTERS

Left to right: Ross Gortner, Narver Gortner, Vernon Gortner,
Hugh Marjoe Ross Gortner

CHAPTER 1

 *She sat the three-year-old in a tiny club chair with a flowered print slip cover. He squirmed for a moment until he nestled obediently into the seat. Then he stared at his hands, which he kept clasped in his lap. She gently lifted his chin with her hand until their eyes were level. The intensity of her gaze warned him that what was happening was important.*

Seated across from him she began reading aloud a four-minute sermon. Then she explained the Bible verses it was based on, and asked him if he understood. He shook his head. She read the sermon again, repeating each line over and over. Then he repeated each line after her, not in his natural voice, but in a chesty roar, imitating her perfect diction. In twenty minutes his attention lagged.

Lifting him by the seat of his pants she took him to the kitchen sink and let cold water run over his head. He was gasping for breath when she turned off the tap, dried him, and put him back in his little chair. The reading-repeating session began again. In a half hour his gaze wandered. She lifted him again, took him to the sofa, and held a pillow over his face until

1

he begged to go back to his chair. After the first day, punish-
ments were no longer necessary, and she trained him five hours
a day for four weeks. Finally the child had perfectly memorized
his first sermon. Her future sat before her. Her way out.

Vernon Gortner was a man who would always have, especially when he was dealing with the have-nots. He understood
their wants and fears, their desires and dreams, and he made
them his business just as they had been the family business for
three generations. Vernon was a Pentecostal minister, and
religion was his trade.

Even in his thirties, before his shoulders crumpled forward
into his chest and his beaklike nose drooped further over his
mouth, Vernon could not have been considered a remarkably
attractive man. Yet what he lacked in physical appearance he
made up in charm, a charm that brought congregations flock-
ing to his church every Sunday. In the 1930s, when ministers
were starving all over the country, Vernon was not. He lived
in a large house in Jamaica, Queens, with the wife he had
married when he was nineteen years old. He owned his own
church, the Calvary Tabernacle, and made wise investments in
large parcels of land in Huntington, Long Island. In his community he was admired: a deeply religious man from an impressive religious background.

Vernon's grandfather, Ross Gortner, was the first minister
in the family, a stern-looking gentleman with a pointed beard.
As a Methodist minister his work involved him with the famous missionary Bishop Taylor. In 1888 Ross Gortner, his

wife, and their fourteen-year-old son, Narver, accepted an invitation from Bishop Taylor to join him in saving black souls in Liberia. Taylor was a respected religious figure and the invitation a prestigious one—a deadly one, too. A few months after the party arrived in Liberia, a malaria epidemic spread through the missionary campsite. Ross Gortner died in three days. Narver buried his father next to their tent and Bishop Taylor erected a plaque which read GORTNER—1888.

Narver and his mother immediately returned to the United States, where Narver himself was ordained a Methodist minister. He eventually became known as an excellent speaker, and even gained a reputation as a fairly good poet. A few years after his return from Africa, he had married and settled in Omaha, Nebraska, where he became pastor of the McCabe Methodist-Episcopal Church. A son, Vernon, was born in 1903. The Gortners had lived in Omaha for only five years when Narver was offered a pastorship at Calexico Church, outside San Diego, and the family moved to California.

At the turn of the century a new phenomenon emerged in American religion that was radically to affect Narver and the entire Gortner family. During a prayer service at a small church in the West, a fourteen-year-old black boy fell to the ground in convulsions and for some minutes babbled fluently in an unknown language. The incident was reported and discussed in churches throughout the Midwest. Those who chose to consider it a religious experience attributed it to an "infilling of the Holy Spirit." Supposedly this was the Pentecostal gift of tongues, described in the Acts of the Apostles.

> And they were filled with the Holy Ghost and began to speak
> with other tongues, as the spirits gave them utterance.

But many religious figures regarded the incident as a prank or trickery.

In 1914, years after the first reported incident of "speaking in tongues," Narver attended a prayer camp in the redwood forests of Cozadero, California. Prayer camps provided for intense sessions of worship, interrupted only for food. Narver, who was still a Methodist at the time, secluded himself in the attic of the little bunkhouse where the camp members slept. The room was hot and still. After several hours of relentless prayer, Narver felt his body begin to twitch spasmodically. Without losing consciousness, he keeled over and began to "speak in tongues."

The possession of his body by the Holy Ghost was the most overwhelming experience Narver ever hoped to attain as a spiritual man. He saw it as the turning point of his life. That same year, 1915, he became a Pentecostal, and in 1919 joined the Assemblies of God Church, which had been founded four years earlier.

From the time Vernon Gortner was twelve years old he was surrounded by the fervor of his father's new religion, and there was never any doubt that he would follow in his father's footsteps. In 1922, when he was nineteen, he left his parents and moved to New York to study for the ministry. The following year he was ordained by the Eastern District Council of the Assemblies of God Church. He opened an independent ministry in Brooklyn, and called it the Lighthouse Tabernacle.

4

Vernon met a kindly and docile woman, and married her in 1922. For the next eighteen years he emulated his father's devotion with gratifying results. His success, in part, was due to his charm, but there are those who still say bitterly that his achievements were due chiefly to his love of money.

Vernon was well aware that no matter how potent a minister he might be, he could not by himself draw sizable financial offerings from his flock week after week. He studied trends carefully. In the late 1930s a new wave of evangelical activity spread across the country. Evangelists were becoming stars, just as in the entertainment industry, and Vernon brought the stars to his church.

Marge McMillan was such a star, if not of the first magnitude. She was a woman of striking beauty, a statuesque blonde with charismatic stage presence and a lively act. She and her hard-working young partner, Leone Blonde, billed themselves as the "Canadian Sisters," although their only connection was professional. Their trademark was the white tailored suits they wore. The costume was Marge's choice, and the handsome pair was admired and envied by congregations throughout North America. Their popularity was based largely on their attractiveness and on a sermon that Marge had made famous within the field, "From Wheelchair to Pulpit." It was heartrending, and entirely untrue.

As the adopted daughter of the Reverend H. Stuart McMillan, Marge had been brought up rather strictly. Her father had very definite ideas about a woman's place, and often quoted the Bible to her: "Let your women keep silence in the churches: for it is not permitted unto them to speak; but they are com-

5

manded to be under obedience, as also saith the law." This conservatism, however, failed to influence Marge. She grew up independent, headstrong, and determined to be an evangelist.

In 1940, when the Canadian Sisters were booked into Vernon Gortner's church, Marge's ego and her desire for national fame were in full bloom. The engagement was for two weeks only, but it was enough. The end of the two weeks saw the end of the Canadian Sisters, Vernon's marriage, and his ministry in Brooklyn. While Marge informed her partner that they would no longer be working together, Vernon informed his wife and children that he was leaving. Marge's long blond hair, piercing blue eyes, and superb figure had dazzled Vernon, twelve years her senior. She was also a woman of exceptional intelligence, and Vernon had no second thoughts about giving up his dull life to run away with the vivacious girl. Thirty years later he was to admit wistfully, "I never loved a woman more than I loved her."

They went directly to Las Vegas and settled there to await Vernon's divorce. Marge, twenty-five years old, was in a schoolgirl flurry. As soon as they rented a small apartment, she called her parents to tell them she had given up her career. They weren't especially displeased that Marge wanted to marry, but when she told them that Vernon would be divorced, they were horrified. Surely Vernon would be excommunicated from his church. Marriage to a divorced person was unheard of in the McMillan world. They wrote to Marge, begging her to give up her plans and return to the road with Leone Blonde. But she paid no attention, and could not, in fact, understand why such a fuss was being made. Vernon was established, and rich, and would make an excellent husband. She was taken aback, however, when she received a letter from Vernon's children asking her not to marry their father. They warned her that the marriage was doomed. "What kind of man," they wrote, "would desert his wife and four children?" Marge ignored them all. They were a perfect pair, and Vernon was an excellent partner with whom she would continue her career.

The divorce was followed by their marriage and, quickly, by Vernon's excommunication. Then the unforeseen began to happen. The settlement broke Vernon financially. He signed the house over to his children. His ex-wife demanded massive alimony and was granted it by the court. Vernon sold the property he owned in Huntington and sent her the cash. Not very long after they had first met, Vernon and Marge were living in a rented house in Long Beach, California, penniless and wondering what had gone wrong.

In later years Marge would value her anonymity, but in the early 1940s it was a curse. After she had tended house for a few weeks, her predicament unfolded before her. Instead of going on to greater triumphs, she seemed to have left fame and success behind. Vernon was shocked at her unhappiness. He had never promised her fame or riches. He believed, innocently enough, that she had married him because she loved him. It didn't matter to him *how* they lived as long as they were together. Yet it mattered to Marge. It mattered a great deal. During their first few months together Vernon was distressed to notice her attitude changing. There was only one way for him to make a living that would satisfy Marge, and, disregarding all the warning signs he was well equipped to read, he incorporated a new Pentecostal church in Long Beach, retaining his ministerial title.

While the newlyweds were enacting their private drama, the nation itself was in the midst of a far greater one. But if the Gortners were aware of the impending war, they gave no indication of it. In the past, Vernon had been faced with many problems in opening and running a church, but none like those he encountered in 1941. They took all his time and attention. Yet, despite his efforts and experience, if not to his entire surprise, the new church was a failure.

Perhaps Marge suffered most from wanderlust. An evangelist is a traveler, and there was no road ahead with Vernon. He made frantic attempts to book them into local churches as guest preachers, and he often succeeded, but guest preachers appear only once, and that was not enough to satisfy Marge's need. They would have left Long Beach to follow the gospel trail, but World War II frustrated those hopes too. Gasoline was rationed and automobiles were prohibitively expensive, if available at all. Every possible exit seemed to lead to a cul-de-sac. Finally, when they were both in a state of deep depression, Vernon took a job selling Watkins Liniment.

The J. R. Watkins Company was located in Winona, Minnesota, and billed itself as the "oldest and largest company of the kind in the world." They sold extracts, spices, and toilet preparations—a far cry from spiritual salvation. Yet Vernon applied his remarkable gifts as a salesman to his new enterprise, and within a short time he became a distributor and opened a small store in Long Beach. Grudgingly, Marge worked in the store while Vernon sold door to door for extra cash. The other salesmen liked the jovial ex-minister, and no one objected to dealing with his beautiful and charming wife. The Watkins Company found the Gortners a great asset.

For some, the life the Gortners were leading could have been a happy one. Vernon's distributorship expanded rapidly and once again he had money. A secretary, Flo Laverne, was hired to help Marge with the paper work. Within a year they bought their own oceanfront home on a palm-lined street, and Marge acquired a maid named Nadine. Life was comfortable, but none of it satisfied Marge's yearning.

She was alone in the Watkins store one afternoon when a young man walked in the front door with a pistol in his hand. They faced each other across the counter: the man was obviously nervous and Marge watched him with her usual aloofness and self-assurance. She waited for him to speak. He didn't seem to know what to say to the pretty blonde behind the counter, and minutes passed. Finally, in a barely audible voice, he asked her for all the money in the store. Marge looked down at the pistol and smiled sweetly. "I have one of those too," she told him, bending down to reach for a gun that didn't exist.

The young man blanched and ran out the door.

Despite her heroic behavior on this occasion, Marge refused to return to the store. She sat alone in the house, watching Nadine clean and becoming increasingly discontented, and when, after a few weeks, she realized her sit-down strike was not having much effect on Vernon, she began to argue with him continually. Vernon tried cajoling and promising: the future would be different; as soon as the war was over they would be out on the road again. But there was no end of the war in sight; Hitler was marching across Europe; and that meant one thing only to Marge: no evangelism. Unable to alter circumstances, Vernon could only continue to book all the preaching dates he could find in the area, and he tracked down a woman minister in Los Angeles, Essie Binkley West, who could, he thought, help them. Mrs. West was an austere woman in her fifties who was known as the "Angel of Skid Row." She administered food and religion to the down-and-out at her Sunshine Mission, and she had also attracted national attention with a "Girls' Town" she had built in Riverside, California. Her Church of the Old Time Religion had a large regular congregation and attracted even bigger audiences for special preachers. After Marge and Vernon had made friends with her, they were booked for a few meetings.

But the sparkle and flair of the Canadian Sisters had gone by now. Up on the stage, Marge and Vernon attracted little interest. Vernon performed well as a Sunday minister but he couldn't carry the show as an evangelist. They had no gimmick, no fish hook with which to grab their audiences. After a few meetings Mrs. West canceled their appearances.

Marge became frantic for a way out, and Vernon grew more panicky every day. He too had given up his life and success for this marriage. He could not afford another divorce and, beyond that, he wanted to keep Marge with him. There was an ancient formula for dealing with restless wives and, without discussing it with Marge, he adopted it.

In May 1943, Marge became pregnant. Vernon waited confidently for her to come back from the doctor's. When she did, she was in a rage. A child in her life would almost certainly destroy any chance of returning to the road. A child would cripple her; she didn't want it. She sat at home for months and thought about her alternatives. She might conceivably prevent the child from getting in the way of her professional life, but there were thousands of evangelists on the road, and she was no longer one of the Canadian Sisters. What would be her gimmick? Could the baby fit in?

The answer was obvious, but the scheme so far-fetched that Marge tried—without success—to put it out of her mind. If stardom was lost to the mother, perhaps it could be recaptured through the child. If the baby was a girl, perhaps her life could be patterned after Marge's own. She spent the last months of her pregnancy trying to figure out a name for the baby. She wanted it to be an extraordinary name; Vernon wanted a family name. Marge won out. The girl would be called Marjoe, a combination of Mary and Joseph. Vernon, not so positive as Marge that the baby would be a girl, settled for contributing the middle name, which, he insisted, would be Ross.

On January 12, 1944, Marge's labor began. It lasted almost fifty hours before the doctors performed a Caesarean section. Shortly before the decision was made to use surgery, Marge insisted that Vernon summon Dr. Charles Price, a respected local clergyman, so that he could dedicate the child to God at its birth. When the baby was finally taken from the womb, the cause of the long labor was discovered. The fetus had become entangled in its own umbilical cord, and the tiny infant was nearly strangled by the cord around its neck. The obstetrician told Marge it was a miracle the child had lived. In her drugged state she asked him to repeat what he had said. It was an omen.

11

The birth of her child was a gift from God, a sign from the heavens. Her way out. And this revelation was so overwhelming that Marge quickly forgot her disappointment in giving birth to a boy.

Hugh Marjoe Ross Gortner was born on January 14, 1944, and from his first breath Marge and Vernon knew there were big things in store for them all.

For the first time in four years Vernon began to relax. Now that the baby was here, there was no discussion of whether or not he was wanted. Marge held court in their home. She told everyone the same story. Her child was a gift from God. His birth was a near tragedy that had become a miracle. She stood by the crib for hours, lightly touching the baby's sandy hair, distressed by his large ears and blaming Vernon's family for them. She bought a flowing white dress for his christening and allowed Vernon to carry him proudly though a maze of friends and relatives. Marge Gortner had produced a Miracle Child, and now she had to find a way to make the rest of the world believe it too.

He was treated, from the start, as a gift of God. She took him with her everywhere. Before he could even sit up, he was attending church meetings with his mother. Before he learned to say "mama" and "papa" he was taught "glory" and "hallelujah." With Marjoe in her arms, Marge paid daily visits to churches where evangelists were featured. She introduced him to ministers as if he were an adult, while they in turn looked down in wonder at the infant in her arms. She wheedled her way onto radio talk shows and brought the baby with her. When he was nine months old she had already trained him to shout "Glory" into a microphone.

Shortly after her son's second birthday Marge arranged for him to have baton-twirling lessons. Another ambitious mother might have arranged French lessons for her child, but Marge wanted Marjoe trained in an art he could display. He had to meet the timetable for greatness.

Clark Higgenbotham was the local band instructor and baton-twirling teacher. For a year he worked patiently with Marjoe, teaching him drums and saxophone as well as the baton. It was the first test of the child's abilities, and he met it astoundingly. After a year had passed he was ready for his next step, the accordion. To teach him Marge found Rocco Legett, a music teacher vaguely connected with a local symphony orchestra. She arrived at every lesson with a heavy terry-cloth towel and spread it across Marjoe's legs so that the folds of the accordion wouldn't bruise his thighs.

If Marjoe's training was extreme, the little boy never realized it. He was carefully kept apart from other children, and there was thus no way for him to learn that his life was unusual. He may not even have realized that other children existed, but if he had it would have made no difference. He was told, nightly, daily, that he was not just another child. He was miraculous, above other children, blessed by God and here on earth with a mission.

When Marge became pregnant again in October 1945, she had some hope that the child would be a girl. But in view of Marjoe's progress, the new baby was unlikely to have anything but secondary importance in her life. During the last months of this second pregnancy, Flo Laverne, Vernon's loyal secretary at the Watkins Company, and a devoutly religious woman, accompanied little Marjoe on his busy schedule. On June 19, 1946, Marge and Vernon became the parents of a second son, also by Caesarean section, and named him Vernoe.

Marge seemed to consider Vernoe's birth as no more than an interruption in the diction lessons she was giving Marjoe. She felt it necessary to clear away traces of his baby talk, and he was taught to project and deepen his frail voice by repeating "All Call for Philip Morris" and reading newspaper headlines aloud. Marge's Scotch Canadian heritage dictated a rolling *r* and she wanted her son to sound like a classical actor.

"Jesus has a special surprise for you," she told Marjoe one night. "You're going to lead his birthday parade."

"What do I do?" Marjoe asked, changing into his pajamas.

"Everybody will dress up in a costume and walk down the middle of the street. They do it for special occasions, and Christmas is Jesus's birthday. We'll have a special costume made for you and you'll walk in front of everybody else and twirl your baton."

She watched as he knelt down by the side of his bed and said his evening prayers. Then she tucked him under the covers and kissed him on the forehead. "Jesus loves you," she told him, and said good night.

Three weeks short of his third birthday, in the scheduled three-mile Christmas parade down Hollywood Boulevard, Marjoe made his first public appearance. Marge had designed a rhinestone-studded baton which had been made to order so that he could twirl it easily. He held his head high with pride as he pranced through the streets in his white satin tailor-made trousers and blouse, white tassels on his boots, caught up in the excitement of the crowds. Marge ran along the periphery of the parade to make sure he wasn't swamped. Higgenbotham marched directly behind Marjoe, leading the Elks band, and from time to time Marge thought there was something strange about his high-stepping walk. She noticed too that Marjoe kept glancing behind him. At the end of the parade she found the seat of Marjoe's white pants covered with footprints. Even the made-to-order baton had proved too heavy for the three-year-old to keep aloft on the long march, and Higgenbotham had inspired Marjoe to keep twirling by a succession of kicks.

What a three-year-old wants most from its mother is love and security. Marge was Marjoe's only source of both, and he soon became acutely aware that memorizing the words his mother repeated to him was of the utmost importance. If he satisfied her by learning them, he would be rewarded with the warmth of her embrace. The penalty for forgetting was just as clear. It was straight Pavlov, and was to affect all his subsequent relationships.

His only friend was Nadine, the family maid. She slept in a tiny room in the basement, a room that eventually became a haven for the boy. He was allowed inside only in the mornings, when Marge gave Nadine her insulin injections, but every afternoon he would sneak downstairs and hide in the room while Nadine snorted a handful of snuff, even though he knew Marge had once caught her at it and forbidden her to keep

15

tobacco in the house. Nadine's gentleness and the fact that she made no demands on him made it possible for him to confide in her and to share her secrets. Then, too, there was the physical pleasure he associated with her, for at Marge's insistence it was Nadine who bathed the two little boys and rubbed them down with oil so that their young skin would stay soft and supple.

Marge had become intimate with Flo Laverne. The Gortners had originally met Flo at a Pentecostal church meeting, and when Vernon first hired her as a secretary, their relationship had been strictly formal. But when Flo stepped into the breach to take Marjoe on his rounds during the months before Vernoe's birth, she became a close friend and confidante of the family.

Flo and Marge wanted to do something to make the boy look more ethereal, and one morning they approached Marjoe.

Marge was holding a small brown bottle.

"I've got a wonderful gift for you!" she told him.

"You'll look just like a little angel," Auntie Flo promised.

Marjoe looked suspiciously at the amber bottle.

"Do I have to drink it?" he asked.

Marge and Flo looked at each other and smiled.

"No, no. Wait and see."

Marjoe, a bit frightened, followed them to the sink. He held his nose for nearly an hour while the two women peroxided his hair. When they were through, his scalp was burning and he raced to his parents' bedroom, climbed up on a chair, and looked at his reflection in the mirror. He began to pout. Tears rolled down his face. His hair, now a brassy blond, hung limply around his head. Two large ears protruded from either side.

"Marjoe!" Marge said from the doorway. "What's the matter?"

"I look silly!" he cried. "Take it off!"

Marge lifted him off the chair, took him back to the kitchen, and gave the new locks a home permanent.

The reading-repeating sessions increased in length and intensity, and Marjoe was not too surprised when Mom-Marge told him he was soon to repeat what he had memorized in front of a large group of people. Flo served as his first test audience. When she applauded, Marge was ready for the big time.

After a year of preparation, rehearsing, dyeing, and polishing, and just a few weeks after his fourth birthday, the Gortners rented Symphony Hall in Los Angeles and invited the local press to attend their gospel meeting. Marjoe, Vernoe, their parents, and Flo Laverne piled into the family car and drove to the hall an hour before the scheduled meeting. On the long ride Flo played games with the boys, trying to keep Marjoe diverted. But Marge insisted on his repeating the six-minute sermon half a dozen times in the course of their journey. At the entrance to Symphony Hall, she took Marjoe's hand and led him up the front steps into the huge auditorium. Up on the stage a handyman was arranging a microphone and podium before the empty hall. From the trunk of the car Vernon produced a twenty-six-inch pulpit, freshly built and painted, and set it next to the tall pulpit on the stage. Marjoe sat in a chair and waited.

An hour and a half later, the auditorium was full of well-wishers and curiosity seekers. Marjoe twisted uncomfortably in the wooden chair as flashbulbs popped in his face. Vernoe cried so loudly that Flo Laverne had to wait with him in the car. Vernon started the meeting, Marge followed him, and then they invited the little boy to the front of the stage. He repeated his lesson word for word. He said he had had a vision in his sleep. He had seen thousands of people crying to him, begging his help, and he had answered, "What can I do? I'm only a little boy!" and Jesus had spoken to him, telling him to spread His Holy Word. The next day small photographs and stories appeared in newspapers in New York and Los Angeles: it had been an amusing incident on a busy day. Then all was quiet again.

Marge and Vernon waited for the world to beat a path to their door, but a four-year-old delivering a six-minute sermon was not outrageous enough to create the kind of attention they wanted. What the family really needed was a professional to champion their cause.

Louis P. Wolfe joined the staff of the *Chicago Tribune* in 1920. The *Tribune* was owned by Colonel Robert McCormick, a man who liked splashy news and big scoops, and Wolfe broke into the newspaper business under his reign. Almost two decades later the *Tribune* transferred Wolfe to California as their Los Angeles correspondent. Shortly after arriving on the coast, Wolfe impressed the home office by scooping every paper on the retirement of General Douglas MacArthur. Nineteen forty-eight was time for another big Louis Wolfe story.

Wolfe first read about Marjoe in the local papers. He met with Marge and Vernon to explore the possibilities of a better story, but they were at a loss for ideas. What could be more interesting than a four-year-old delivering a complicated sermon? What about a four-year-old minister? Wolfe suggested. Marge loved the idea but Vernon doubted it would be legal. Checking the California state laws, Wolfe found there was no age requirement for ordination. Although the Gortners both retained their own ministerial authority and hypothetically could have ordained Marjoe themselves, they knew the validity of the child's status would be questioned. Whoever ordained Marjoe had to be strictly legitimate, preferably well known, and, most important, had to believe there was a sound reason for ordaining the child.

Replacing the youngster in his miniature club chair, Marge carefully explained that no one must know his mother had taught him his sermon.

"How do I learn it, then?" Marjoe demanded.

"You don't learn it. You just say it," Marge told him.

"What do I say? How do I know what to say?"

"Jesus tells you," Marge insisted.

"Jesus! Isn't Jesus in heaven, Mom-Marge?"

"Yes. But Jesus is everywhere too. And he tells you to give your sermons."

"How?" the little boy insisted.

Marge thought this one over. "When you nap. In your sleep. Just like in the dream where the people were calling to you."

"Don't I get tired, then?"

"No. Not when God speaks to you in your dreams. Just

remember this: when you go to bed and close your eyes, Jesus gives you thoughts for your sermon. And you don't memorize them. They're extemporaneous."

"They're what?" Marjoe asked.

"Extemporaneous." Marge made him memorize the word.

Marge and Vernon hustled the boy off to Essie Binkley West, the perfect person to perform the ordination. She had heard about the little boy but she was somewhat dubious.

"Why do you want to preach, Marjoe?" she asked.

"Jesus tells me to preach."

"How does he do that?" Mrs. West asked.

Marjoe glanced knowingly at his mother. "In my sleep. He gives me sermon thoughts. Then I say them extemporaneous."

Essie Binkley West listened to the boy preach and immediately agreed to ordain him. No matter how he got the material for his sermon, his preaching convinced her he was a very special case.

Marge and Vernon had arranged for six children in tinsel angel wings to grace the altar of the Sunshine Mission for the ceremony. Mrs. West was horrified to see so many members of the press present, especially a certain Louis Wolfe from the *Chicago Tribune*, who seemed to be in charge of the proceedings. Nevertheless, on Halloween, October 31, 1948, dressed in flowing white robes, she ordained Marjoe with "all rights and privileges of the ministry as given by our Lord Jesus Christ" while he stood before her in Fauntleroy velvet and satin. Wolfe sent the story and photographs to the *Tribune*. In the days following, Vernon visited every newspaper in California with a press release and photographs.

The press treated the ordination as a freak. The great publicity stunt was regarded as a stunt. California's reputation for weirdness offset the sincerity of the four-year-old preacher. Although the story made the front page of some papers, it blew over in two days. Two months went by. Marjoe spoke at a few meetings. Marge began thinking again, and she asked Louis Wolfe to their house.

What could a four-year-old minister do that was more outrageous than being a four-year-old minister? Wolfe suggested that he do what every minister does: perform a marriage ceremony. Marge loved the idea. She assured Wolfe that Marjoe could carry it off with dignity. If Wolfe arranged it, he would get exclusive coverage, but this time the Gortners wanted the event boosted into a national news story. That included newsreels and radio. Wolfe agreed, provided the whole event was legal.

Vernon pored through the California laws again. Again there was no age requirement necessary in order to perform a marriage ceremony. Any ordained minister could do it. Marjoe went into another period of intensive training to learn the ceremony and prepare for a press conference.

Using the reading-repeating method Marge had developed for his first sermon, Marjoe memorized the entire Episcopal marriage service. The Gortners excitedly informed Essie Binkley West that Marjoe desired to "join a couple in holy wedlock." She said No. She saw no point in allowing the ceremony in her church. The boy's anointing was to win souls for Jesus, she insisted, and nothing else was necessary until he was older.

As the person directly responsible for his ordination, she felt it would be a misuse of his ministerial powers.

Vernon located an unsuspecting Virginia West, who was in no way related to Essie Binkley West. Virginia owned a small marriage chapel in Long Beach, and because she thought it was a cute idea she agreed to allow the boy to perform the ceremony at her church. Wolfe, in the meantime, began a hunt for a sympathetic couple. Long Beach was a busy naval port in 1948, and Wolfe scoured the docks for a sailor wrapping up a whirlwind romance. After three unsuccessful days he realized he was at the wrong place and headed for the Long Beach license bureau. In an hour he had located freckle-faced, red-haired Alma Brown, age twenty-one, and Raymond Miller, age twenty-three, a seaman first class on the U.S.S. *Saint Paul.* The two had met just two weeks before and were at the license bureau to pick up a marriage license before Miller shipped out to sea. Wolfe negotiated the arrangement between the couple and the Gortners, although why the two young people were eager to be married by a four-year-old minister still remains a mystery.

During the short period between Wolfe's deal with Vernon and the actual ceremony, Marge prepared a list of questions that any reporter might ask Marjoe. Jean Harlow's meteoric rise to fame was allegedly helped by a team of bright writers supplying her with double-entendre answers to press conference questions. Marjoe had Mom-Marge to write his.

On January 4, 1949, in the Normandy Chapel, Marjoe nervously raced through the wedding ceremony in his strained child's voice, peering up at the couple with frightened eyes.

Present were some fifteen people, including his parents, Vernoe, Virginia West, Flo Laverne, Alma Brown's sister, and Louis Wolfe with the Paramount Newsreel cameramen. Marjoe wore his black velvet suit with white cowboy boots. The moment he was through he said, "Raymond, kiss ya bride!" Raymond did. Marjoe let out a huge sigh and made national headlines.

COUPLE WED BY 4-YEAR-OLD MINISTER
4-YEAR-OLD MINISTER TIES FIRST MARITAL KNOT
4-YEAR-OLD L.A. PARSON WEDS PAIR

Virginia West was furious with the Gortners. The event made her chapel seem seedy and cheap, like a Las Vegas marriage mill. The exclusion of reporters other than Louis Wolfe confirmed her sneaking suspicion that they were all publicity seekers. Alma Brown's sister was said to be "disgusted." So were the American clergy.

The *Los Angeles Times* ran a story and picture on page two, headlined CLERGYMEN RAP WEDDING RITES BY CHILD MINISTER. The secretary of the Church Federation of Los Angeles, Dr. E. C. Farnham, called the ceremony "a violation of good taste." Dr. John MacArthur, pastor of the Fountain Avenue Baptist Church, said, "As far as I'm concerned it's disgusting!" Then the clergy everywhere began to question the legality of the marriage. When the ceremony was shown nationally in newsreels, the attorney general's office of the State of California found it necessary to reply. They quoted Section 70 of the California Civil Code, which the Gortners already knew. It read: "Marriage may be solemnized by either a justice of the

Supreme Court, justice of the District Courts of Appeal, judge of the Municipal Court, justice of the peace, judge of any police court, city recorder, priest or minister of the gospel of any denomination." Everyone was amazed that the State of California had no age requirement. Rabbi L. Groffman hoped public opinion would "condemn this unfortunate practice as being a dangerous and harmful precedent."

Marge and Vernon were on their way, and the press was not about to let a good story die. On January 6, the *Los Angeles Mirror* ran a new headline:

OH MY SON, MY SON!

Mrs. Nova Miller, the groom's mother, grieved in her home in Springfield, Illinois. Mrs. Miller said she would try to persuade her son to have the marriage solemnized in the Catholic Church. Alma Brown had other ideas. "I think that in the eyes of God we're as legally married as though God himself performed the ceremony." Her reply sounded as though Marge was writing for her.

On January 12, Marjoe was ready to hold a press conference. The NEA wire service carried the story, headlined: HOW CAN THEY CONDEMN ME? ASKS MARJOE GORTNER, 4-YEAR-OLD PARSON. The reporters assembled in the Gortners' living room, where Marge and Vernon made short introductory speeches before presenting Marjoe. His opening line was "How can they condemn me when Jesus set a little child in the midst of the Pharisees to teach them?" He went on to inform the shocked reporters that his sermons were not memorized, but that Jesus gave him themes for them in his sleep, just as he had seen

24

thousands of desperate people crying to him for help. A monsignor had remarked that Marjoe was "as incapable of witnessing a marriage contract as Charlie McCarthy," and one of the reporters asked Marjoe what he thought about it. "Who is Charlie McCarthy, Mummy?" Marjoe asked. Marge laughed embarrassedly and gave him a prearranged signal to end the press conference. Marjoe left the room.

The literal icing on the cake appeared two days later on Marjoe's fifth birthday. In answer to all the criticism and wailing, Raymond Miller and his new wife flanked Marjoe as the newspaper cameras captured him blowing out the candles on a birthday cake. A few months later, in a Kansas City paper, Vernon Gortner made the most audacious comment of all. "They wanted the boy to marry a couple in a prizefight ring," Gortner was quoted as saying, without specifying who "they" were, "but we refused. Too much like a publicity stunt."

Louis Wolfe received the following telegram from Seymour Korman of the *Chicago Tribune*. "Tell Louis Wolfe the following notice is on the bulletin board: 'Louis Wolfe is hereby awarded a bonus of $50 for discovering and bottling up the story and pictures of the Los Angeles boy preacher, a nationwide beat.'"

The following year, at a meeting of the California state legislature, a law was enacted which set twenty-one as the minimum age for ordination and for performing a wedding ceremony. But it was too late. A nine-year odyssey had begun.

ON THE ROAD

CHAPTER 2

Marjoe ran down the cellar steps and knocked on Nadine's door. "It's me, Marjoe," he called, hoping she wouldn't hide her snuff.

Nadine opened the door and looked down at the little boy.

"Well, well. My little preacher man."

Marjoe walked into her room and sat on the chenille spread covering her bed. "We're going across America." he told her.

She rubbed her hands together excitedly. "I know, I know. You sure are gettin' famous." She laughed and sat down next to the boy.

"Will you come with us?" he asked her.

"No. I got my own family to stay with. Your mommy's gonna get somebody else to go with you."

Nadine opened the top drawer of her dresser and unwrapped a fresh can of snuff. Marjoe watched her apply the tobacco to each nostril and snort noisily. She wiped her hands on her apron and sat back on the bed.

"I guess I don't envy you, though. It's no happiness for a baby *your age to be goin' through what you been doin! Lord help you!"*

"Worldly parents make their children movie stars. Why shouldn't my parents make me a star for Jesus?"

One month after his fifth birthday, the parents of the "World's Youngest Ordained Minister" announced a national pilgrimage. The Associated Press carried the story on its wire service, which informed an uninterested nation that Marjoe would be on a "barnstorming gospel tour" in Texas, Arkansas, Missouri, Iowa, Kansas, and Colorado before returning home. The Gortners never returned home. Vernon shuttered all the windows and draped the furniture in white sheets. Marge took her hand-painted china out of its display cabinet and wrapped each piece in newspaper. For the next nine years Marjoe would be out on the road, preaching, performing, and conning millions of people across the country. Middle America was about to be treated to entertainment they would remember for years. In exchange for their dollars, Marjoe brought the glamour and sparkle of show business right to their front doors.

Marge and Vernon understood evangelism well enough to know they would have to make the "big kill" on the gospel circuit in the first few years. Other evangelists used techniques that would be effective for a long time, building popularity year after year. But Marjoe would only grow older; the initial impact of the Miracle Child would inevitably diminish. They planned a relentless pilgrimage.

They set out in a Buick "Woodie" station wagon with their

30

sons and two chihuahuas, Bambi and Blueboe. Because there was so little space, most of their possessions were left in storage. Later they would buy a large trailer to tow behind the Buick, but for the first year on the road the family lived in a succession of hotels and motels.

Vernon headed the publicity department of the gospel caravan. Under Louis Wolfe's tutelage he had learned the mechanics of advance publicity. A Chicago advertising agency was commissioned to help him. Wolfe himself had become concerned that his connection with the Gortners might endanger his job at the *Tribune.* His newspaper would have considered his activities highly unethical, unless he was promoting the family's antics out of love, which was doubtful. In a letter to Vernon in June 1949, Wolfe urged him to be discreet about the relationship. But, in fact, after arranging the publicity in a few cities himself, Vernon no longer needed Wolfe's assistance, and the newspaperman quickly faded from their lives.

Vernon's publicity work followed the same pattern in every town. First he settled the family in a hotel or motel. His frugality always led him to the cheapest of accommodations, distinguished by the pervasive odor of frying food, but Marge hated these places and insisted that they stay in quiet and dignified hotels. Vernon would help the family start a few meetings, then drive to the location of their next booking, often several hundred miles away. There he would complete arrangements for an auditorium, secure accommodations for the family, and call on the entertainment editors of the local papers. The editors consistently greeted Vernon with the same response. "You don't want to advertise on the entertainment

31

page, Reverend. Why don't you speak to the religion editor?"

"No, thank you," Vernon would tell them. "Godly people read the religion page. We're after the sinners, and they're all in your section of the paper."

The advertisements Vernon placed in the paper were colorful reproductions of Ripley's "Believe It or Not" cartoon of Marjoe. The oddity-hunters at Ripley's had been presented with the drawing by gospel artist Clarence Thorpe and delightedly included it in their archives. The place and date of Marjoe's meetings were slugged across the bottom of the cartoon. Vernon ran additional advertisements in the comic strip section of the Sunday papers. He preferred these ads to appear after the "Katzenjammer Kids." His strategy was that on Sunday people read the funnies only, and a Marjoe cartoon was a perfect way to attract the Sunday sinners. Finished with the advertising editor, Vernon dropped in on the news editor, promising he would be back in a few weeks with a fascinating story.

Marjoe was prepared with increasing care for the self-promoting news conferences Vernon had arranged. When they arrived in a town, Vernon and Marge would take him directly to the newspaper offices. Any reluctance to write a story about Marjoe was handled by the little boy's boldness. He introduced himself to reporters with a manly handshake and a condescending "God bless you," and then, without pausing for breath, he would launch into a carefully rehearsed monologue about his motivations in that city.

"I'm here to give the devil two black eyes," he would begin, his fist thumping a wall or desk. "We need more good Christian mothers and fathers who don't drink horrible cocktails and suck filthy cigarettes. They're giving their souls to booze when they should be giving their souls to Jesus!" The reporters, city editors, and onlookers would be amazed. Was this tiny man really only five years old?

"Show them some of my press clippings," Marjoe encouraged his parents. Then the Gortners told the story: Jesus gave him sermons in his sleep; the boy had been anointed by the Holy Spirit; he had preached to over fifty million people in a year. When the interview was about to end, Marjoe would prod the newspapermen: "Don't you want to take my picture preaching?" Often they did, after which the five-year-old blessed everyone again. "Give us a good write-up now," he said, shaking a finger at them as he left. His story always ran on the front page. City to city, year after year, the free publicity brought overflow crowds wherever Marjoe spoke. Filling a four-thousand-seat auditorium was an easy task.

Marjoe would arrive at the auditorium just before his performance time and find hundreds of people waiting outside to see him. No matter what the weather, there were always people there, in pouring rain or freezing cold. His bookings were always for two weeks. He held a meeting each night, with a matinee added on Sunday. Mondays were reserved for traveling to the next location.

The people in Marjoe's congregations idolized him, and returned every night the Miracle Child was in town, bringing friends and relatives with them. It was important, and showmanlike, that the Gortners had variety and sparkle for each and every performance. By the end of his first year on the highways

Marjoe had a working list of seventeen different sermons in his head. Memorizing was a full-time job, six to eight hours a day, reading and repeating in hotel rooms and, later, in the trailer. Marge wanted each sermon letter perfect. One slip could betray that they were not spontaneous. Hence, every element of the show was rehearsed; Marge even taught Marjoe how to shake hands with his flock so that his fingers would not be bruised.

Marge told her son which sermon he would preach a day ahead, but there were occasions when the sermons were changed at the last moment. Marjoe was at his pulpit one night when Marge rushed over and told him to preach an entirely different one. She had spotted a newspaper reporter in the audience, and was afraid he had already heard the scheduled sermon and might expose Marjoe's supposedly spontaneous preaching. The startled little boy stood before an enormous audience trying to figure out what sermon to substitute. Uncomfortable seconds passed until the first words he needed came into his head. He learned to be prepared for anything.

Performances began to follow a rigid pattern. While a small choir sang onstage, the audience would begin to fill the auditorium. The people who came to see Marjoe duplicated themselves all over the country. The vast majority were from the blue-collar segment of white America. Many of them were poor and uneducated. There were factory workers and field hands. Most had never been to a live "show" before. They could not afford television, and radio was the most spectacular form of entertainment they had available. But now they had Marjoe. When they came to see him they dressed in their

Sunday best, their children following them down the aisles in droves, as if they were attending a circus. The parents herded their offspring in with relish. Little girls wore flouncy party dresses, while their brothers squirmed uncomfortably in ties and jackets. The adults came to see Marjoe from a mixture of curiosity and hope and hunger for an experience transcending their burdensome daily lives. The children were there to stare at a miraculous child touched by the Holy Spirit.

The choir sang until the auditorium was full. Then Marge and Vernon mounted the stage. Vernoe accompanied Marge if he was in good enough humor, for the younger child was shy and moody. He suffered from frequent nervous stomachaches, and often remained backstage or hid in the trailer. Vernon addressed the audience first, introducing Marge and the visiting clergy. Marge continued to wear the white suits she had made her uniform when she was a Canadian Sister. The men and women out front fell quiet with envy and admiration as she was introduced. To them Marge was a modern-day Mary, yet as glamorous as a movie star. Vernon was charming and witty at the microphone. He told his spellbound audience the hackneyed story of Marjoe rushing up to the pulpit and announcing he was a preacher also. He described Marjoe receiving sermons in his sleep. Finally, when he felt the crowd could endure the tension no longer, Vernon suggested a little entertainment, from the Miracle Child himself. Marjoe was always calm at the moment of his introduction, and remained at ease throughout his performance. Although it had not yet occurred to him, he *was* a performer, and he knew his act well.

Middle America was about to be impressed with a display

of musical talent they found astounding. Marjoe sang and played hymns on every musical instrument he had learned, in rapid succession. His job at this point in the meeting was to engross his audience, then to fire them. He implored everyone to sing along. He excited them into clapping. His voice filled the air, crisp, high, sometimes squeaky, and his rolled *r*'s gave him a strangely compelling quality. It was not a little boy entertaining: it was a grown man. Jesus behind a mask.

His twenty-six-inch pulpit stood at the front of the stage next to his father's tall one. Marjoe dragged an enormous Bible up to the white stand and flung it on top, opening it at random. He held the complete attention of the crowds, whether he faced several hundred or several thousand. With a deep breath he launched into his sermon, his gestures perfectly choreographed to his words. He paced the stage, knelt on one knee, or lifted his huge, imploring eyes to the heavens and invoked God to come to these people. "Tonight we're going to chase that mean old devil right back to Hell! My call to you is a last call and a warning! When God anoints a little child he is using drastic measures to gather others in ere it is forever too late!" His sermons were spine-chilling forewarnings of hell and damnation. Ten feet behind him his mother watched, seemingly enrapt, shouting out "Hallelujah"s and "Amen"s. In this way she was able to give the little boy his signals unnoticed. "Amen"—slow down; "Oh, Jesus"—speed up; "Oh, God"—gesture more; and finally the one the family liked best, "Hal-le-lu-jah!"—take an offering!

Vernon directed the first collection of money, which ended Marjoe's sermon. Marjoe went to the back of the stage and sat quietly with his brother and mother. The first year on the road the Gortners thought it would be best to keep him uninvolved in the direct collection of money. When the first offering was over Vernon usually picked an element of Marjoe's sermon and ad-libbed on it. Alternate nights Marge might deliver a short sermon. Then a second collection was taken, and finally an altar call, at which Marjoe officiated. A count of the people who came forward to be individually blessed was made at each show. On the following evening the number would be exaggerated and exploited. The actual number of people was unimportant to Marge and Vernon, but it did give them an indication as to the type of crowd, how strong their beliefs were, how reticent they were about participating, and how the take could be improved on the following nights. They found that the more individuals who came up to the altar, the more money Jesus would bless them with.

Marge kept Marjoe on a perfect diet, filled him with vitamins, and made sure he had enough exercise for a growing boy. But Marjoe had learned early that her love was, in other respects, conditional. If he gave an exceptional series of performances, perhaps delivering a particularly difficult sermon, she would buy him a toy. Yet the toys and games were transient; when the family moved from place to place, the toys were left behind to save space in the station wagon. He never had a playmate, except for his brother. He was expected to act and react like an adult at all times, but he was hardly allowed the sympathy or forgiveness an adult might expect. On rare occasions, in an affectionate mood, Vernon would take the boy to a nearby amusement park to ride the roller coaster. Between engagements they would have a game of catch, or a day's fishing, but Marjoe never felt real tenderness, the kind Nadine had given him, from either parent.

Within a short time the Gortners realized that changing Marjoe's sermon each night did not offer enough variety to keep the crowds returning, especially when the family played the same towns and cities year after year. The solution was "Theme Nights," and if as evangelists they had narrowly missed appearing to be a circus or a vaudeville act, the addition of themes certainly came close to burlesque.

The most natural theme for the family, and a popular one with the crowds, was Western Night. Marjoe customarily traveled in hand-sewn cowboy boots made of kid. His name was appliquéd in gold across the front of each boot, and the sides sported a flashy golden cross. On Western Night, Marjoe walked onstage twirling a lariat, another art in which he had been tutored. For his opening he sang an "original" composition called "Roundup Time in Glory," to the tune of "Home on the Range." The pulpit was now a tree stump, which Vernon kept in the rapidly growing prop department in the trailer. At Marjoe's right lay an artificial campfire, complete with electric light and whirling tin foil. The back of the stage was ringed with a little barbed-wire fence, and a real saddle sat on a construction horse next to the tree stump. The sermon was entitled "Heading for the Last Roundup" and brought a warm response in western cities. The "Last Roundup" was so popular, in fact, that Marjoe accepted numerous invitations to preach to cowhands on huge Texas ranches, including one meeting at Will Rogers' old ranch. No one seemed to notice

38

that Marjoe repeated the service verbatim each time he delivered it.

Modern cowboys were carefully differentiated from the old-time shoot-'em-up genre since cowboys and guns were considered evil by the Gortner family. Marjoe was forbidden to watch television programs that involved firearms or violence, and this created another problem for the boy, whose favorite program was "Hopalong Cassidy." Roy Rogers even invited Marjoe to appear on his weekly TV show, but Marge and Vernon refused, informing the surprised Mr. Rogers that his show was not Christian enough for their son. Ironically, one of Marjoe's best lines at news conferences was "I'm here to get the boys and girls to hop-a-long to Jesus."

The "Illustrated Sermon" was Marjoe's favorite. This was not only a night to preach; he could be a real magician and dazzle his congregation with the magic tricks his father had arranged for him. He was presented onstage with a five-foot-tall plywood heart. From behind little doors in the heart Marjoe produced a fish bowl of water. "This bowl," he announced enthusiastically, "represents your heart when you are born. Clean! Pure! But then comes the devil and sin!" Marjoe produced a vial of chemicals and began adding it to the water. "Then your heart gets blacker. Smoking . . . blacker; drinking . . . blacker!" Finally the water turned completely black. Then came Jesus, the Saviour, who was in another little vial Marjoe added to the fish bowl, which turned its contents clear again. Following the transformation, Marjoe produced a giant piggy bank from behind the red heart and took up an offering for Jesus.

The themes often bordered on the ludicrous. When Marjoe talked on the "Bread of Life" he wore a baker's costume and a huge white hat. For biblical stories of David, the shepherd boy, he was resplendent in an Oriental costume. Wednesday nights were always called the "Miracle Restoration Service," at which Marjoe made feeble attempts at faith healing. (In a short time, however, his healing techniques were to improve, as that facet of evangelism became more profitable.) His sixth, seventh, and eighth years were highly profitable for the boy preacher, yet it was a precarious period as well. He lived on the brink of exposure.

No matter what theme or sermon Marjoe worked with, the basic thrust was toward giving to Jesus. Thereby the Gortners would receive. In "Come to the Stable," a favorite Theme Night, with Marjoe in shepherd's costume complete with staff and stuffed lamb, he would say:

> I may be only five years old, but my Jesus means more to me than any old Santa Claus. I thank God for a Christian mother who had enough Christian character to get me acquainted with Jesus and tell me the truth about Christmas when I was a mere baby. Make room in your hearts for my Jesus! He loves you boys and girls. How it must grieve his great heart of love when you forget his birthday. Won't you please give Jesus a gift this Christmas? . . . Oh, yes, there's plenty of room for gifts, gifts for Grandma. . . .

Marjoe's preferred night, above all others, was the night Mom-Marge preached "From Wheelchair to Pulpit," for that night Marjoe stayed home and watched Hopalong Cassidy. But he missed quite a show, for Mom-Marge was still a spectacular

40

speaker, and Saturday nights were always allocated to her famous sermon.

Marge began Saturday night by singing. Vernon would then join her in a gospel song before Marge launched into "Wheelchair." The sermon began with a detailed account of a car crash in Canada. Marge is hurtled through the front window. She sees the glass splintering around her as a useless life flashes before her eyes. Awakening in a somber hospital, she is informed by the doctors that the splintered glass has severed her spinal cord. Marge went into great medical detail to give the story credibility. The accident left her paralyzed from the neck down. Life became misery. She had to be fed and cared for. The ultimate degradation was her inability to use the bathroom alone. Her thoughts turned to suicide. She wanted nothing but death, yet her crippled state prohibited even that option. Finally God appeared before her, and called her to preach. God made a deal with Marge: the pulpit in exchange for the wheelchair. But Marge even fought with Jesus! She refused him for months and languished in bed. Jesus was not one to give up easily, and in the end Marge promised to dedicate her life to his work.

The crowds went berserk over Marge's eloquent recital. Offerings rustled forward in large denominations. On Saturday night Marge was the star, and that, after all, was what she had wanted from the start.

The first three years of the fifties were the best for the Gortner family. Not only did they progress through a series of expensive trailers; they were able to buy their own three-pole tent. The acquisition of the tent allowed the family to appear at almost any location. The trailer was transformed into a dressing room at the site, while the Gortners set up headquarters in a nearby motel.

It was shortly after the Gortners had bought their tent and a truck to haul it that Forrest Potter joined the caravan. Potter presented himself to the family after a meeting in South Carolina and offered his services, free of charge. Vernon needed someone to drive the truck and pitch the tent, so Potter was added to the group. Naturally he received no salary, but in a short time he made his interests known. Potter was an amateur artist, and wanted to make religious drawings to sell at meetings. His artistic talent was of great importance to him. He received tremendous satisfaction from drawing and having people see his work. Vernon ingeniously incorporated Potter's art into meetings on Family Night, when he was featured in the performance.

Much advance publicity was given to Family Night. Vernon promised that the largest single family in attendance would be awarded a very special prize. At the beginning of the sermon Potter played "What a Friend We Have in Jesus" on his "gospel" saw. Then he sat by an easel and began a pastel sketch of a heavenly house beyond a flashy rainbow. Marjoe spoke of the "Foursquare Golden Home in Heaven" while Potter, beside him, continued to draw. When the drawing was finished, Vernon asked families in the audience to stand according to the number of members, beginning with the smallest families and working up to families of fifteen or twenty. After much excitement and competition, the largest family was presented with the heavenly view Potter had drawn before their eyes.

Forrest Potter remained with the family for over five years. Such people were useful to Marge and Vernon. Although they hired a new maid, Mandy, in a small southern town, they needed extra help. Parishioners, devotees, and religious zealots made themselves readily available. At the end of each meeting someone was always around the trailer begging to join the caravan. Jesus had told all these people that their mission in life was to join the Gortners on their pilgrimage. Most often the Gortners refused, judging carefully who should be thus privileged. For a while Marge's parents traveled with them in the trailer, but when they tired of life on the road and retired to Dallas, Texas, the Gortners decided to replace them.

The first set of gospel groupies to travel with the Gortners were the Reverend and Mrs. George Van Hoover. The Van Hoovers claimed to have traveled as assistants to evangelists Billy Sunday and Paul Rader. Anxious to get back to the road, they were allowed to dedicate their lives to Marjoe and his family, following them around in their own car. The hood of the car was equipped with a three-foot neon light which blinked "Youth for Christ." Atop the car's broad roof a four-sided marquee, triple-rimmed in neon, announced "Marjoe, World's Youngest Evangelist! In Person. Age 5." The trunk was adorned with a two-foot-tall mock-up of the Holy Bible. At each town George would stand on the street corners from morning to night handing out circulars for Marjoe's meetings. Mrs. Van Hoover baby-sat for the two boys. When they left the Gortners after several years' servitude, they presented their car as a gift.

The Van Hoovers were followed by the Reverend and Mrs. John Poe, a childless couple in their late thirties who were relentlessly devoted to the Gortners. The Poes arrived at a meeting in Saint Petersburg, Florida, and after hearing the little preacher lay down the gospel, offered their services forever. Brother and Sister Poe received no salary, but their expenses—mostly money for gas—were paid.

All the couples selected to join this unique fan club were treated very formally by Marge and Vernon, and the Gortners presented these people in an interesting light to their other fans. Marge wrote about it in 1950:

> We all travel by trailer and oh what a blessing these ministers of God are in our services. . . . There is so much to do in these large services and these willing workers help wherever they are needed, but best of all they are great prayer warriors and are our ministers in charge of the altar service. Marjoe throws out the Gospel net—these great warriors of the cross help to bring it in. . . .

An odd threesome called the Happy Sign Trio joined the caravan for nearly a year. Geraldine, Jane, and George provided musical back-up for the family in their early tent meetings. But before they were allowed to join the entourage Marge cross-examined the three on their relationship. Geraldine and George were married. Jane was George's sister. They lived together in their own trailer and Marge found the situation respectable enough to allow them to accompany her family. However, the association between the trio and the Gortners was quickly severed when Marge discovered the three asleep in the same bed.

At campsites the attendant couples were asked to park at a respectful distance from the Gortner trailer. Marge and Vernon insisted upon this distance, for the private activities of the family were not for outsiders' knowledge, especially the long rehearsals and memorizing sessions to prepare Marjoe's sermons. The Poes and Van Hoovers devoutly believed the sermons were extemporaneous, a faith that must have been severely tested in view of their constant repetition.

These couples protected and chaperoned Marjoe on the rare occasions when his parents were not nearby. If Vernon was in the next town and Marge was busy shaking hands with the crowds, they guided their precious ward to shelter. In their company, Marjoe was careful to keep up the "blessed child" behavior they expected.

The Gortners had patrons who admired them from afar, a situation free of entanglements and consistently profitable. Brother and Sister Wainwright were an Ohio couple who intermittently joined the Gortners on their travels. He had been a manufacturer of enamel paints for refrigerators and, after making his fortune during the war, had retired shortly before Marjoe began his road tour. Pressed by the boredom of wealth, the Wainwrights would turn up in every fourth or fifth city. They'd take the family out to dinner, offer a generous cash gift, and disappear again. In this way they were able to hobnob with the Gortners and other prominent evangelists of the time. The relationship offered the Gortners money, friendship, and the use of the Wainwrights' home and influential connections in Cincinnati.

Brother and Sister Cooper were from Charleston, West Virginia, and they carried their patronage one step further. The competitive Coopers would alternate towns with the Wainwrights. Beyond the lavish hospitality they bestowed on the Gortners, Sister Cooper's expert skill with the needle was an additional benefit. Marjoe's extravagant costumes were a chore for Marge. His growing body changed shape every few months, and since it was Marge's intention to keep Marjoe in costume at all times, even between appearances, his complete wardrobe was Liberace-like in its complexity. Sister Cooper loved the responsibility of Marjoe's costuming, and under Marge's careful direction she became the seamstress for the little boy. Marge designed the outfits and Sister Cooper executed them by the hundreds, at not one penny's cost to Vernon and Marge.

Marge must be considered an expert at recycling, as well as a mastermind of resourcefulness. She met a man who was Marjoe's biggest fan . . . and fetishist. Every day for nearly four years the gentleman mailed two dollars to a post office box in Long Beach, over seven hundred dollars annually, in return for Marjoe's old clothing. The man's letters graphically described how he displayed the precious articles in his home. If Marge and Vernon thought the fellow a little strange, they kept it to themselves. Two dollars a day made his desire for old clothes a religious act.

The longest, fondest, and most profitable patronage of the Gortner family came from Brother and Sister Cole, in Memphis, Tennessee. They first met the Gortners at a Memphis meeting in 1949, introducing themselves by personally presenting a check for one hundred dollars. The hundred-dollar figure became the Coles' trademark. It was offered to the Gortners each and every time they were in each other's company, even if that happened several days in a row. Marge and Vernon visited the Coles frequently, their travels bringing them through Memphis often. On these occasions, along with their regular offering, the Coles insisted that the Gortners partake of a gospel dinner with them.

Dinner at the Coles' was an event Marjoe dreaded. Up on a stage he felt secure, but sitting in someone's home he was vulnerable. If he was asked a question he had to have the perfect answer. His manners were under careful scrutiny. He hated these intimate encounters.

The Coles' maid would reverently greet the family and usher them into a large sitting room where Brother and Sister Cole awaited their arrival. The phonograph tinkled gospel tunes and hymns. Marjoe and Vernoe would sit uncomfortably on the sofa, waiting for their turn to entertain, while Marge and Vernon talked about a new sermon Marjoe had been given, or how many souls had been offered to Jesus and saved by the young preacher since they last met. Finally Marge would produce one of Marjoe's musical instruments, usually his accordion, and for half an hour Marjoe played and Vernoe sang. When dinnertime finally arrived Marjoe was all set to plunge in ravenously, but first he had to thrill the Coles by saying grace. During dinner Marge kept a watchful eye on him, kicking him under the table to correct his manners, making sure his knife was turned in at the side of his plate and that he chewed with his mouth closed. After dinner, fortunately, a good deal of the feast would be wrapped for the Gortners to take away with them. A hundred-dollar check would be presented at the door, and Marjoe would be on the road again.

How much money the family collected or where it went will always be open to conjecture. Funds were collected either in person at meetings, or through the mail to the "home office" post office box which Flo Laverne attended to in Long Beach. When the Gortners first left California, they asked Vernon's secretary and Marge's confidante to continue working for them by running all the Marjoe enterprises.

Flo not only handled the correspondence for the family, but compiled a widely circulated book called *Marjoe—A Modern Miracle*. The cover portrayed the little boy patriotically posed between two American flags. The first edition, published in 1948, was filled with photographs of the tot in dramatic Billy Sunday poses. It contained a much censored account of the Gortner family history, including articles on Great-Grandfather Gortner and Marge. The book glorified Marge and made frequent reference to her as an ex-Canadian Sister. Although Marjoe was not old enough to write, many of the articles were attributed to him. Many others were reprints of laudatory reviews. Some stressed Marjoe's unending popularity, and noted the numbers of people who had to be turned away from every meeting. The book promoted Marjoe and his spiritual powers to an outrageous degree, but it was surprisingly low keyed in soliciting money. The need for dollars to spread the gospel may have been referred to throughout, but there was never a flagrant demand. The last page was an advertisement for another pair of Marjoe promotions.

The first of these was called *Twilight Tidings*—"the only newspaper in the world published by a six-year-old." Subscriptions were just a dollar a year, but the mailing list of names was more important to the business than the profits from *Twilight Tidings* itself. Flo Laverne was editor of this "newspaper" also. She published the first issue in November of 1950. *Twilight Tidings* was purely an advertising mailer for the Gortners. In four or five glossy pages it included the text of Marjoe's most famous sermons, rehashings of stories from *Marjoe—A Modern Miracle,* and a separate column by Flo Laverne called "The Children's Corner." Flo's sideline in *Twilight Tidings* was called the Gospel Drama House. Through it she sold religious plays she wrote for schools and churches. The mailer's back page included Marjoe's itinerary and a plea for money to pay for the tent, which cost over fourteen thousand dollars. Most of the page, however, was devoted to an advertisement for the second venture, Marjoe record albums. The albums were initially recorded at the Sacred Records Studios in Los Angeles, but as Marjoe's sermons multiplied, tapes were made on the road and incorporated into the set.

On their first visit to the studio, Marge explained to Marjoe the purpose of the recording sessions. "These records will reach thousands of people. Many will be saved for Jesus. So just pretend you're in a big room and preaching to a lot of people." The engineers were shocked when they saw the little boy stand

49

calmly before the microphone and let loose with a twenty-minute diatribe on sin. Marjoe himself was more fascinated with the boom microphones and sound effects than he was with recording an album. His recorded sermons turned out to be surprisingly dynamic, and became a potent dollar-earning tool.

Flo Laverne never received a salary for her endless work. She was a believer—in Christ and in Marjoe. Although she was perfectly aware Marjoe's sermons were memorized, and although she herself wrote some of them, she continued to believe the boy was blessed. She is credited by some with having written the most popular and astounding of all Marjoe's sermons, "Hell with the Lid Off," a frightening, almost bizarre foreshadowing of the relentless tortures of Hell. Its complete text ran thirty-five minutes, and halfway through parishioners would be throwing themselves on the altar. A twelve-minute version was immortalized on a Marjoe record album, his voice rasping out the hideous terrors awaiting sinners below. Twenty years after its premiere, both Vernon and Marge claim authorship of the piece, for it stands as a tribute to the power of the little evangelist.*

There was a constant flow of letters to Flo from the family on the road containing vivid descriptions of Marjoe's speaking dates. She was told that all the auditoriums were packed, thousands were turned away each night, hundreds were healed, but there was no money. Notes to Flo enclosed new subscriptions

* See Appendix.

to *Twilight Tidings* and some letters included a twenty-dollar bill or some other small gift to keep her working.

A letter Flo received from Vernon in 1949 instructed her to sell the Gortners' Long Beach residence for nine thousand dollars. The letter went on to tell her that they had been able to book the city auditorium in Montgomery, Alabama, which seated over three thousand people. Yet, Vernon continued, "Auditoriums have been so high here that we have made nothing—just broke even—so while many have been saved it has been a hard time financially." The following paragraph instructed Flo to write letters to the Chamber of Commerce in thirty-nine cities to find available auditoriums. The Gortners were indeed so successful on the road that they literally did turn away thousands, but Flo Laverne never got to share in any of the rewards.

If it was money and fame that started the whole thing, it was money and fame that would end it. After a short time on the road all that the Gortners thought about was how to get the most money out of the crowds quickly. When they appeared in a local church a split was decided upon with the pastor. Often a percentage was worked out. For example, if a pastor claimed that he needed four hundred dollars a week to keep his church running and produce some salary for himself, the Gortners might split sixty-forty with him on everything collected above that amount. When the Gortners rented their own auditorium, or worked out of their tent, everything above cost was straight profit.

All monies collected were supposedly used to spread the

word of Jesus, and only one night a week did the Gortners tell their audience that the collections were being taken for themselves. A Love Offering was a collection taken as a personal gift. On the night of a Love Offering it was made clear that all other monies collected went to expenses and the dissemination of the Word, but the Love Offering was for the adorable blond-haired little boy who stood before them, so that he could eat, could have clothes to wear, and could enjoy a toy that he and his brother might play with. To finish the plea, an actual piggy bank was produced instead of the usual ice cream buckets that were passed through the crowds. Vernon bought these banks wholesale, by the gross. After each Love Offering, Vernon would splinter the bank with a hammer, while Marjoe watched its green and silver contents ooze from inside.

Only with Love Offerings did Vernon allow Marjoe to count a handful of pennies. The rest of the cash collected was almost never counted in front of Marjoe or Marge. Vernon would presumably take the money out to the trunk of the car, or hide it somewhere, until he had a chance to count it away from his family. Marjoe overheard frequent arguments on the subject. Marge accused her husband of opening clandestine savings accounts across the country and making deposits in every city. At times she would be furious at his keeping secrets from her, but she was angrier still at his stinginess. It was she who insisted that the children wear the most expensive clothes and stay in the best hotels. Vernon, she said, would have been satisfied to put the family in some fleabag.

Even when their congregation exceeded five thousand people, Vernon still refused to give Marge any money. It was then that she began to badger him about it in the presence of the sponsoring pastor, and went so far as to stage noisy scenes in front of the congregations. "You're not going to get the money out to the trunk this time!" she would scream at him, and Vernon would angrily hand her enough cash to quiet her for the moment.

With the purchase of the tent, the traveling evangelists played more rural areas, where their customers returned night after night without much money. Therefore the second night in farm country was declared Grocery Night, and the donations accepted would include food. The industrious wives of the farmers would prepare dozens of turkeys and homemade pies in lieu of cash, and the bushels of fruits and vegetables were uncountable. Grocery Night kept the family eating in the trailer for at least three weeks.

Money was only one of the problems Marge and Vernon began to encounter. The size of their family had mysteriously increased. On a spring day in 1950, in Charleston, West Virginia, the Gortners had a special surprise waiting for Marjoe and Vernoe. A tiny baby girl lay in a crib in the trailer. Marge told both boys that she and Vernon had just adopted the infant. Since the Charleston meeting was being sponsored by a minister who also ran an orphanage, Marjoe assumed it had been scheduled to fit in with his parents' plans for adopting another child. But he was puzzled by the fact that neither Marge nor Vernon had ever revealed their intention.

"What's her name?" Vernoe asked, staring into the crib.

"She was the brightest star in the heavens," Marge told him, "so we'll call her Starloe."

Starloe's sudden arrival was treated casually in the next issue of *Twilight Tidings*. It said, ". . . PRESENTING "STARLOE!" The rest of the article follows:

SIX YEAR OLD REV. MARJOE GORTNER
DEDICATES STARLOE FRANCINE
GORTNER

The First Baptist Church of Sturgeon Bay, Wisconsin where "The Old Rugged Cross" was composed, January 12, 1913, was the setting for one of the most touching scenes ever witnessed. People sobbed over the entire audience, a capacity crowd jammed into the Historic church where Rev. Hulbert is Pastor. Dr. George Blomgren Dewey, noted news analyst and one of the former preachers of the Country Church of Hollywood for 2 years was present.

When she was old enough, Starloe was trained to sing with Vernoe. Just once was she allowed in the limelight, when she was featured on the front cover of *Twilight Tidings*. But after that the "brightest star in the heavens" faded into the obscurity Vernoe had lived in for years.

Vernoe had been nicknamed Sugar-baby, and he hated it. Yet the rest of the family continued to call him that, especially Marjoe, who taunted him with the cruelty that siblings typically inflict on one another. Marjoe never dared talk back to his parents, and Vernoe was the only person around on whom he could unleash his aggressions. Furthermore, Marjoe set incredibly difficult standards to live up to, and all the Gortner children were judged by their preaching ability. The longest sermon Vernoe was able to memorize lasted only six minutes, and he was allowed to preach it only twice. He intoned it like a child instead of a midget, and that quickly put an end to his career.

The Gortners never neglected their younger son, but no one was ever really interested in him. He wasn't the breadwinner. He had no talent. He was an average little boy who had had the misfortune to be born into a family of stars. He pouted sullenly at the back of the stage or nestled in his mother's arms at meetings. In hotels and trailers he would sometimes batter his head against the wall and chant "Dumb Sugar-baby, dumb Sugar-baby. . . ." There were nights when he smashed his head against the wall with such force that he had to be restrained.

The show must go on, and relentlessly it did. Occasionally the religious three-ring circus crossed the paths of a real circus. In Canton, Ohio, for the first time, the Gortners found themselves pitching their tent on the parade grounds occupied by the Mills Brothers Circus, seating five thousand people. Competition with a circus could have been disastrous for a revival meeting, but Vernon knew how to turn every situation to his advantage. He not only scheduled Marjoe's evening performance to begin a half hour after the circus ended, but in every opening parade Marjoe rode high above the others atop Big Burma, "the world's largest elephant." He never forgot the thrill. At first a stepladder was placed at the elephant's side for Marjoe to mount to its back, but Marjoe desperately wanted to be lifted by the elephant's trunk, just as the professional performers were. Initially Marge forbid this. Her son was too precious to allow so dangerous an exercise. But after many hours of practice and pleading Marjoe persuaded her to relent, much to his delight. High on Burma's back, he held his right hand on his hip and waved to the crowds with his left, riding down the main street of Canton in total bliss. The ringmaster would announce the Miracle Child and his revival show.

"There he is, folks, the Miracle Child! The lame walk, the blind see, the deaf hear, the dumb speak, and he's only just down the midway!"

Marjoe was entranced by the circus and its carefree performers, and he reveled in being allowed to join the acrobats and animal tamers for meals under the big top. His parents were just as happy as he: through the cooperation of the Mills Brothers they were able to double attendance at their meetings.

Constantly in search of new ideas, they were soon to find that radio was an increasingly easy way to raise money. In the early 1950s Marjoe pretaped a series of programs that were broadcast over WGRG in Louisville, Kentucky, the Gortners' home away from home. The program was known as "Calvary's Call," and the response to Marjoe's aggressive voice over the air was most impressive financially. The entire family joined in the radio show, which allowed them to reach thousands of people who were unable to attend meetings. A large segment of the radio response came from the seriously ill and bedridden who had to turn to Jesus through the media. Letters were received daily at a Louisville post office box. The mail speaks best for itself. The following letter was written in pencil, the writing on an eighty-degree slant:

Dear Gortner family
I will write you again. I am still a faithful listern. I am allways around the radio when the time comes. I love Jesus I trust Jesus will heal my eyes. I blieve on Jesus. I want Jesus I Dont go to the Dr. now Jesus is my Dr.

Another letter received the same day is reprinted here in its entirety:

Pray for me. That God will save my soul and heal my sick body

The Gortners marked in red on the outside of each envelope the amount of the donation it contained. A picture of the Gortner family was sent the donor; a copy of *Marjoe—A Modern Miracle* if the donation was large enough. All the names were added to the *Twilight Tidings* mailing list for future use.

THE PROFESSIONAL

CHAPTER 3

 During the five years the Marjoe road show had been in business it had prospered. The Gortner conglomerate operated through record albums, radio, pamphlets, calendars, personal appearances, and a school for infant preachers called "Marjoe's Mission," which never even existed.

When Marjoe was seven he was considered experienced enough to estimate how much a particular crowd was worth, and he was allowed to lead the offerings. If he was working in a large auditorium, in or near a city, he would start by asking for the largest amount first.

"Twenty dollars! Twenty dollars for Jesus. Let Him come into your hearts. Can I have ten twenty-dollar bills so Jesus can help save a sick world?"

The first bills were always easy to get, the rest were slow and tedious. At times Marjoe would stand before the crowds begging twenty-dollar donations for as long as half an hour. Then the ante would drop to ten dollars, and so on.

Also, when Marjoe was seven, the Gortners noticed how anxious their congregations were for physical contact with the

61

little star. Children were awed and frightened by the anointed boy, but their mothers and older sisters appeared to be strongly attracted to him. Conscious of this, Marge would announce that twenty dollars for Jesus would bring a kiss from Marjoe. Because Marjoe hated this system of raising money, and complained about it often, Marge reacted by springing it on him unannounced. Then he would wander reluctantly through the crowds, the pressure of their bodies making him miserable. Yet, after spending some minutes on the floor, he would try to make the best of it. "I've got one!" he would yell to his mother, waving a twenty-dollar bill in his hands. There would be laughter from the crowd and, in another moment, another bill. Allowing Marjoe to accept the offerings personally became so profitable that Marge had deeper pockets sewn into his pants.

Tucker Jamieson was a minister in Dallas, Texas. He weighed nearly three hundred pounds, balancing his weight on little legs as he scurried across the stage, waving a long white handkerchief that he produced from his back pocket. His handkerchief was more of a prop than a necessity, although the huge man perspired constantly. But Jamieson's effeminacy did not affront his parishioners. His mincing only added to the weekly shows. His regular congregation ran from eight hundred to a thousand people, who rocked with religious laughter when Jamieson screamed "Whoops, Shaillot!" instead of the usual "Hallelujah!"

Jamieson's wife and two daughters lived with him and attended every meeting, while his boyfriend, Artie, was kept in a small apartment across the city. Sister Jamieson was an attractive woman in her early thirties, with wavy brunette hair and a large bosom. It was she who precipitated the only occasion in Marjoe's career when he forgot a sermon. It was her habit to seat herself in the audience across from the little preacher, and, as he delivered his sermons, she would make long sweeping motions crossing and uncrossing her legs. During one particular sermon, she didn't bother to twine her legs at all, and Marjoe's roving eyes traveled past her garter belt to her pantyless crotch. He stood behind his miniature pulpit speechless. Marge signaled "Oh, Jesus" to him frantically. Finally he launched into the second half of a different sermon, finished quickly, and rushed off the stage. Mom-Marge plagued the boy with questions, but he refused to explain his lapse of memory.

The Gortner family not only preached in the Dallas church often; they also spent four Christmases with the Jamiesons, and when they could they returned to Dallas for the summer meetings. During the last few days of one particular summer meeting, Vernon left to do publicity work in the next city while Marge and Marjoe finished their booking in Dallas. Following the meeting, Marge remained out front to shake hands with the eager congregation, and Jamieson took Marjoe back to his large air-conditioned office. After he counted out the evening's take, he told Marjoe an involved joke about two prostitutes. When Jamieson delivered the punch line, Marjoe only stared at him.

"Little sweetness," Jamieson said, "what ever is the matter?"

"What's a whore?" Marjoe asked.

Jamieson explained. "Do you know what a fairy is, blessed

one?" Marjoe shook his head, and Jamieson detailed a joke about a homosexual, a Texan, and an umbrella. The conclusion of the story led to Jamieson exposing himself and then beginning to undress the little boy. Fortunately before he proceeded further, Marge appeared on the scene. Wisely she made no fuss, but it was a long time before the Gortners would again see the fat flaming preacher and hear his screams of "Whoops, Shaillot!" Jamieson eventually divorced his wife and became a full-time roommate of his friend Artie.

The constant repetition and boredom of the road mingled with an odd feeling of unfulfillment to make the entire family restless. This increasing discontent pushed Marge and Vernon further apart. Vernon appeared to be on his good behavior when he was with the family. But what went on when he was away was anybody's guess. Marge in turn took advantage of the free time in her own way.

Each night when Vernon was away, Marge put the three children to bed and disappeared. When Vernon returned, noisy arguments ensued. Marjoe listened intently, wondering why his parents were attacking each other so furiously. And questions of money began to worry him. Where did it all go? Why did they argue about it so much? Didn't any of it belong to him? Why, he began to wonder, was it necessary to lie to the newspapers and to the people who came to listen to him and who trusted him? He didn't feel any guilt over what he did, because he understood on the simplest of levels that he was performing for those people, that he even made them happy. But did that mean he didn't have to practice what he preached? Did God allow a public life and a private one too? Yet he knew better than that. He often scolded his flock for being only weekend warriors, for sinning all week and praying to be saved on Sundays. By the age of ten he was asking the ultimate question, "Who am I?" but he did not yet dare ask what was really right.

The more the youngster thought about it, the more he was tempted by the idea of Satan. In secret rebellion, he began saving some of the twenty-dollar bills handed to him by his audience. After all, he was putting on the show, doing all the work. Why not take some of the rewards? Jesus never minded sharing. But Marjoe's petty thievery was short-lived. He became worried, not because he was sinning but from fear of Mom-Marge's anger. Hiding the bills on his person, he accompanied Marge on a shopping trip and escaped her long enough to hand the money away to passing youngsters on the street.

In 1952 Marjoe had reached the peak of his childhood career. He had preached in every part of America, except for the New England states, where his type of evangelism was not widely accepted. In the streets, hotels, and restaurants he had been a certified celebrity. Vernon was a wealthy man, and Marge a successful stage mother. Vernoe grew increasingly unhappy and moody.

But the eight-year-old evangelist was no longer a pretty, curly-haired tyke. He was becoming gangly, far taller than average for his age. His stage manner had become polished and relaxed, and he no longer needed Marge's signals, but he was not the incredible sensation he had been as an infant.

Because his blond hair, endlessly bleached, was damaged and splitting, Marge stopped the permanents and allowed him to comb it to one side in a pompadour. His costumes and cowboy outfits were changed for baggy zoot suits and string ties. They did not enhance his appeal.

With his new hair style, another problem presented itself to the appearance-conscious family. His curls had partially obscured his large ears, but the pompadour seemed to accentuate them, and as his cuteness became awkwardness his ears looked especially grotesque. Newspaper photographs accentuated them. Marge's solution was to put liquid adhesive behind them to hold them back.

She prepared Marjoe before each appearance, holding each ear in place, gluing it down and pressing it back until the adhesive hardened. During the shows Marjoe's perspiration often loosened the glue behind one ear. The congregations would be mystified as the young preacher began to slap the side of his head; it was not to accentuate his words but to loosen the other ear, and often after a sermon his ears and neck would be bright red from all the slapping. It was then that Marge decided it would be best in the long run if Marjoe had his ears pinned back surgically. Marjoe flew to Cincinnati, where their old friends the Wainwrights had recommended a plastic surgeon. After the operation, the tiny stitches pulled behind each ear as Marjoe sat on the plane on his way back to his family.

In an effort to boost the family's falling income, Marge decided to have Marjoe learn more about the lucrative art of faith healing. She took him to watch the greatest faith healers

66

of the time, the three Kirkwood Brothers. Jesse, Andrew, and Frank Kirkwood were from Baton Rouge, Louisiana, all evangelists and each with his own tent. They were hokey country gentlemen, always dressed in elegant white suits. The Gortners crossed paths with the Kirkwoods often, and it was due to Marge's influence on brother Andrew that the Kirkwoods agreed not to hit the same towns at the same time.

Jesse was the star of the Kirkwood Brothers. The two others ran their tents in neighboring states and built their shows for the night brother Jesse would come by and perform miraculous healings. Jesse was a down-to-earth country boy, with a reputation on the circuit for totally draining people of their money. He would prowl through the audience without asking the sick to step forward. But finding someone with a cane or a crutch, he would begin to scream. "It is an insult to come to a Kirkwood meeting with a cane! God's in here!" he boomed at his victim in corn-pone tones. Then he'd grab the cane and break it over his knee. "Get up and walk!" he shouted. From either fear or embarrassment, his victim would hobble a few steps and bring cheers from the congregation.

Marjoe's healing methods were less violent, but every bit as dramatic. His first healings were simplistic: aches and pains that were cured by the firm pressure of his hands on the sufferer's body. While Kirkwood frightened people into recovering, Marjoe turned healing into a mystical experience. People arrived at his meetings already possessed of profound faith. They were prepared to be healed and when they saw the boy, who was clearly an instrument of God, their faith was so intensified that Marjoe had only to touch them to cure a variety of ailments. The young alto voice would project his phrases with deep intensity.

"In the name of Jesus!" he would call. "In the name of Jesus I take authority over you! Dirty, filthy demon! Come out, devil! Hear me now. In the name of Jesus, come out!"

There were times when Marjoe surprised himself. A seven-year-old boy was brought to his tent meeting who had been blind for three years following an automobile accident. The child was led into place in the healing line and Marjoe rushed to the back of the stage to confer with Mom-Marge.

"What'll I do?" he asked her frantically. "He's really blind."

"Heal him," Marge said.

Marjoe cocked his head and stood watching his mother's impassive face. The healing line grew restless at the front of the stage.

"If you believe," Marge whispered, "he will too."

Unsteadily, Marjoe walked to the front of the platform, where two parishioners held the blind boy's arms pinioned to his sides. Marjoe stared into the vacant eyes, hesitating. The blind boy's lips began to move but no words came out. Marjoe leaned forward to listen to his whisperings.

"Heal me, please Jesus. Heal me, please Jesus. . . ."

In a shocking swift gesture, the blond preacher grabbed the boy's head and pressed the palms of his hands into each socket.

"Jesus! Jesus! I beseech you! Heal this boy! In the name of Jesus . . ." Marjoe threw his head back and shouted to the heavens above the tent. His hands turned white from the pressure on the boy's skull. "In the name of Jesus I take authority over these blind eyes and you shall *see!*"

Quickly releasing the boy, Marjoe stepped backward, trembling. The lad teetered uncertainly between the two parishioners. Marge silently watched the blind boy's eyes. The two companions turned him around to help him off the platform when suddenly the boy began to flail his arms about.

"I can see!" he said. "Mommy! *Mommy! I can see!*"

Marjoe was shocked. He glanced at his mother, who stood imperiously by his side. "You can heal," she said to him quietly. "You can heal."

Only one other of the hundreds of healings Marjoe performed as a child surprised him as much as that of the blind boy. A woman arrived at a tent meeting in Iowa with an enormous oozing ulcer on her left cheek. Marjoe was about to touch the sore, as was his usual practice, when Marge sped to the front of the platform. "Don't touch it," she whispered. "It may be infectious." Marjoe waved his hand lightly over the woman's face, chanting his spell, and then turned to the next believer. Two days later the entire Gortner family was astounded when the woman returned with her face completely healed, only a pinkish layer of new skin showing where the ulcer had been.

The Gortners' own physical ailments were attended to by qualified doctors. From time to time Marge fell ill and was forced to return to Cincinnati, where the Wainwrights had recommended a prominent surgeon, George Miller. Marge's bedside counselor was a handsome man in his fifties with a muscular build and a prospering practice. After many years of bachelorhood he had married a beautiful former model.

Marge's first visit to Cincinnati was in 1951, when Miller

operated on a pinched nerve in her right wrist. Her next visit was for her younger son. Vernoe's nervous stomach, left untreated for many years, was severely ulcerated by the time he was nine years old. Marge flew with him to Cincinnati, where Miller operated on the boy. She began to have arguments with Vernon about her visits to Cincinnati. He claimed to have spies in that city who had spotted her with Miller. She countered by accusing Vernon of hanky-panky during his absences on the road. The squabbles might not have turned into anything of consequence had not everything around the Gortners seemed to be falling apart.

The years 1952 to 1955 were critical ones for the young evangelist. There had been a miraculous quality about Marjoe as a child that captured the public and held them spellbound, but now the years were passing the Miracle Child by. Vernoe couldn't inherit the crown. Starloe was ignored. The money began to fall off drastically.

Twilight Tidings was no longer published. The *Modern Miracle* book was obsolete. Flo Laverne took a job to support herself. Bookings were hard to get. Vernon disappeared for longer periods. Marge left the children alone more. The Gortner family was in serious trouble.

Marge was an industrious woman and began to breed toy poodles on the road to raise enough cash to feed the family between engagements. Puppies were born everywhere—in hotel rooms, in the back seat of the car. She dipped them in bathtubs full of green or red dye to enhance their appeal. At the end of each meeting she would announce that Marjoe's dog had littered a few weeks back and that her puppies were for sale. The faithful rushed forward to buy them. But the Gortners were close to being broke. Marge asked one question incessantly: "Where is all the money?" Vernon said there was none. Expenses were high. He told her the same stories he had told Flo Laverne. Marge refused to believe him.

The summer of 1956 was a long, tedious, and unhappy time for the family. The few bookings they were able to obtain were poorly publicized. Vernon couldn't interest the newspapers in the tired old story. He and Marge fought constantly over this. With the proper advertising they could be on top again, she insisted. With a new gimmick they could make a comeback. Vernon turned his head.

The Gortners pitched a tent meeting in Danville, Virginia, toward the end of that sad summer. Vernon left for a few days to see if he could beg another meeting in a nearby city. Marge decided to visit with the minister of a local church, and Marjoe was left with the pastor's sixteen-year-old daughter.

During the afternoon, the young blond girl watched silently as Marjoe climbed a jungle gym in a playground. At three o'clock she suggested that it was time for Marjoe to return to the hotel for his nap. He found the crude maneuvers of the sixteen-year-old amusing. He knew from the moment she looked at him what it was she wanted, and he didn't mind. He was twelve years old, and he wanted it too.

Back in the hotel room, Marjoe stripped to his shorts and climbed into bed. The preacher's daughter, clothed, crawled up next to him.

"Do you know what this is?" she asked, touching her firm breast. Marjoe nodded. "And this?" She ran her hand down the front of her body. The boy nodded again. Enough had been said. She took off her clothes while Marjoe remained motionless on the bed, fascinated. Marge had never permitted the children to run naked anywhere. Finally the girl removed his shorts and examined him appreciatively. Turning on her back, she suggested that the boy mount her. When he had nestled himself into position, he lay lifeless on top of her. He had once spied on his parents, but he wasn't certain about the procedure.

"Well?" she said.

"Well, what?" Marjoe asked.

"Don't let it be a dead fish. Move it in and out."

And thus, with another child of God, Marjoe became a young man.

The next two months brought the family to Savannah, Georgia. Arriving in the city on an Indian summer's day, Vernon hurried ahead to pick up the family mail at a local church. One of the letters was postmarked Cincinnati, with no return address. Although it was addressed to Marge, Vernon opened it, and learned that Miller was divorcing his ex-model so as to marry Marge.

Vernon rushed back to their hotel room in tears. Marge and the children were shocked by his emotional display. He confronted Marge with the letter. "Where is all the money?" Marge demanded. "Why do we have to live like pigs?" It was her only answer.

The argument lasted for weeks, and reached its end in Charlotte, North Carolina, on Thanksgiving eve. Shortly before Marjoe's evening service, Marge returned to the hotel room to prepare herself and her sons for their scheduled show. Vernon should have been waiting in the room. Instead she found a five-dollar bill and a short note on top of the dresser. Vernon had left for California. Marge sat dumbfounded in the empty room with her children, while Forrest Potter waited downstairs to drive the family to their tent.

In Person!

Fe...
IN
BELIEVE
LIFE
an
NEW

I'M ONLY 6 YEARS OLD!

CLARENCE THORPE

Marjoe
"WORLD'S YOUNGEST EVANGELIST"

HE HAS PREACHED TO OVER FIFTY-MILLION PEOPLE !!

...AR AND SEE **MARJOE** PLAY HIS 120-BASS ACCORDIO...
...XAPHONE, DRUMS, TWIRL TWO 'BATONS' AND SING ...
...N COMPOSITIONS; THEN PREACH THE OLD-TIME GOS...
...TIL TEARS FLOW AND HEARTS ARE MELTED. THOUSA...
...VE BEEN CONVERTED UNDER HIS MINISTRY. **MAR...**
...ADE WORLD HISTORY AS THE YOUNGEST MINISTER EVE...
...RFORM A WEDDING CERMONY...

WINDING DOWN

CHAPTER 4

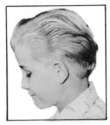 Vernoe tugged at Mom-Marge's sleeve while she reread the note for the third time. Distractedly she patted the youngster's shoulder and told him to play with his brother. Marjoe propped a pillow behind his head and watched her carefully. He had seen Mom-Marge in moods like this before: thinking, plotting, about to make one of her "important" decisions. Finally she folded the note in half and stood up. She walked to the door, changed her mind, and turned to the children.

"Grandmother Gortner is ill," she said, avoiding Marjoe's eyes. "Daddy has left to go see her. Wait here while I talk to Mr. Potter."

Marjoe kept his eyes on her as she turned the doorknob to leave the room. "Daddy always said he'd need onions to make him cry if *she* ever died," he said skeptically.

Potter sat behind the wheel of the huge truck parked in front of the hotel. The foot-tall yellow and red letters were painted across the sides: SEE MARJOE—THE MIRACLE CHILD.

"Mr. Potter!" Marge called up to the cab of the truck. "Where is the Buick?"

"Parked by the tent, Mrs. Gortner."

"And the panel truck?" she demanded.

"Mr. Gortner had it early this morning."

Marge swung herself up into the seat on the passenger side and sat next to Potter. "Mr. Gortner has left for California. The Lord is calling upon his mother."

"Don't say—" Potter began.

"I'll explain more later. This will be our last meeting in Charlotte. After services tonight you'll break down the tent and load it."

"Where to then?" Potter asked.

"I'm not sure. We'll have to decide. But, Mr. Potter, I'm afraid we won't need the tent any longer."

"Does that mean you won't be needing me, Mrs. Gortner?" the man asked.

"I think not, Mr. Potter."

Potter stared out the front windshield.

"You've been a great help to us—your artwork and the tent and all. . . . Take the truck and tent with you, wherever you care to go."

She paused before going on. "You can load all the musical instruments except the organ into the Buick after tonight's meeting. We'll send for everything else later."

"Yes, ma'am," Potter said, staring straight ahead.

Marge went into the hotel lobby and found the classified telephone directory. She made several calls before she succeeded in pawning the Hammond organ. The pawnbroker tried to persuade her to sell it, but that wasn't Marge's style. There was always the possibility she would want it back, in case the family went on the road again. But, in the months to come, Marge was to pawn every instrument Marjoe had so prudently been taught to play.

It was announced at the meeting that night that Vernon Gortner's mother had been taken seriously ill and that the Miracle Child would not be able to complete his scheduled appearances because the family intended to join Reverend Gortner at his mother's bedside. However, funds were low, and Marge, unarguably a genius in such situations, followed Marjoe's sermon with a heartrending plea for money while Marjoe watched from the rear of the platform. The minister of the local church agreed that all collections that night would be love offerings for the entire Gortner family, and when the service ended the congregation rushed forward to wish the Gortners good fortune on their journey to California. In an hour the tent had cleared, leaving only Forrest Potter and the family sitting among the scattered rows of folding chairs.

"I think I'm going to Virginia," Potter told Marge. "To Danville. I once worked the fairgounds there as a maintenance man, and there's probably room to park the truck and tent."

"Good luck to you then, Mr. Potter," Marge said. She handed him enough cash for his journey, arranged for him to keep in touch through the Long Beach post office box, and left him alone in the tent.

Marjoe sat in the front seat of the Buick while Vernoe and Starloe slept quietly in the back. After Marge had driven almost two hours, he rested his head against the back of the seat.

"Where are we going, Mom-Marge?" he asked. "To see Father?"

But he already knew the answer. They were only four hundred miles away from Cincinnati, Ohio.

During the drive to Cincinnati, Marge took stock of their assets. The truck and tent were in Vernon's name and of no use to her. The new 1956 Buick Roadmaster she was driving was also owned by Vernon, but it was in her possession, and she might as well let him make the $175 monthly payments. Realistically, none of it mattered. George Miller was an established man, a doctor. There would be no more faith healings in Marge's family. But of course she couldn't rush into anything. First she would have to find a little house for the children. Then she could surprise George Miller.

Marge had a knack of finding out-of-the-way houses for little money, and the day after they arrived in Cincinnati the family settled into a half-derelict house in the slums.

When Miller heard Marge's voice on the phone he was less than ecstatically happy. Marge herself was enough for the doctor to contend with, but when she told him she was in town with her children and intended to stay, he became alarmed. Still he arranged to see her that night. He arrived at their house and waited outside while Marge gave Marjoe instructions about looking after Vernoe and Starloe.

The children were accustomed to being left alone in hotel rooms or in the trailer while their parents were out, but this would be the first time they were alone in their own house.

Marjoe, just under thirteen, welcomed his new status. When Mom-Marge left them in the Cincinnati house that night, he was not only confident that he could manage perfectly well, but he understood that their roles and their relationship had irreversibly altered.

When the children awoke the next morning, Marge had returned, but Marjoe sensed an unfamiliar tension in her manner. This ordinarily stoical woman, in full control of her life and the lives of those around her, now seemed inexplicably touched by panic. Marjoe's self-confidence increased.

"This house has rats," he told his mother, aware of how upsetting the news would be. "They ran all over the downstairs last night."

Marge suggested that they buy traps and set them up around the house, but Marjoe had a better idea: a BB gun to shoot them with. Marge gave him one of her long hard looks. Her son's suggestion was more than a request for a forbidden weapon. He was serving notice on Marge that he expected her to acknowledge their new situation. With Vernon gone, he was now the man of the household.

"You know what you're asking for?" Marge said. Marjoe nodded, knowing better than his mother that a BB gun would be one small triumph only in the struggle for his own identity. Nevertheless, when Marge capitulated and he got the gun, his joy was a child's joy—true rapture.

After that Marjoe spent his days in Cincinnati wandering through the streets and watching other families. He looked in store windows and wondered about the lives of the people who worked there; where they lived, how their homes looked, what a sense of permanence was like. He often visited the zoo and watched the animals for hours. Afternoons, when school was out, he bundled himself in his overcoat and hurried to one playground or another, absorbed in studying the children, curious to know what it was like to have a friend, what it was like to be one.

It was during an early-afternoon visit to the zoo with Vernoe and Starloe that a man identifying himself as a truant officer asked the children why they were not in school. Marjoe told the officer that his family was just visiting Cincinnati, and that they were enrolled in the Calvert Correspondence School, in Baltimore, Maryland. The children were, in fact, enrolled in the Calvert School, and when there was time on the road, Marge made them study hard. But there had actually been very little time.

Marge had nevertheless educated her sons in her own way. Nothing had ever been secondary to her insistence on evangelical stardom, but her ambition required for them a high standard of breeding, of culture, and of worldly awareness. Her children had been guided through every large museum of art and natural history in America, and had visited historical sites from coast to coast. They may have known little about geometry or literature, but they were not raised to be commoners. They were bred as religious royalty.

Marjoe's authoritative manner and his answer satisfied the truant officer for the time being; nevertheless, their educational program didn't satisfy the requirements of the state of Ohio, and thereafter they stayed indoors during school hours, venturing outside only when they were with Marge. But Marjoe never objected to the temporary confinement. He was able to experience his first Sunday without a meeting. It was the only time he could remember not having to prepare and memorize. It was his first vacation, and the sudden freedom and lack of pressure made him deliriously happy. The house became an amusement park, every room another frontier for discovery. He made up games for Vernoe and Starloe to play. He actually played with Vernoe. He sat by the windows and watched the street, fascinated by the luxury of his new indolence.

Dr. Miller never visited the house the Gortners lived in. He waited outside in his car on the rare occasions when he came to call for Marge. At home Marge never discussed him or her relationship with him, and even Marjoe, with all his astuteness, would not have given it its full importance if he had not stepped on a rusted nail in an old board while he was hunting rats in the basement with his BB gun. The nail went right through the sole of his boot and into his foot.

Marge took Marjoe to Dr. Miller's office. When she announced herself, Dr. Miller's pert young nurse gave mother and son a long deliberate stare. Marjoe noticed his mother's icy calm while they waited with the other patients, and he noticed, too, that the nurse seemed unable to keep her eyes off Marge. When she finally left the room, he whispered to his mother from behind the magazine he was reading, "What's the matter with *her*?"

"Nothing I can't take care of," Marge told him.

The fact was that Marge Gortner was running into quite a bit of trouble with that young woman. Dr. Miller's nurse had been a readily available delight as soon as the doctor had divorced his wife (and probably before). Marge was forty-one, an attractive forty-one to be sure, but it had been long years since she had been in competition with another woman, and this one was nearly half her age. Despite her boast to Marjoe, she couldn't "take care of" Dr. Miller's nurse, and within two months the amorous doctor had completely changed his mind about remarrying, especially into a family of newly retired evangelists. Marge and the children were out.

Shortly before she told the children that they were leaving Cincinnati, Marge pawned the few remaining musical instruments. Then she packed the children into the car and headed for Fort Worth. Marjoe decided not to worry about their destination but to sit back and observe.

When Marjoe was seven years old, their meetings in and around Fort Worth had been haunted by a fat alcoholic named O. B. Crump. Marjoe had first taken notice of O. B. Crump because of his preposterous name, but as O. B. attended more and more meetings, Marjoe realized that his parents were seriously concerned about the man's presence. Once an evangelist himself, Crump had fallen prey to the devil's lure, was usually too drunk to conduct his own meetings, and had tried to latch onto the Gortner family, begging for a place in their entourage. Vernon had been in a panic merely because Crump might be seen in their company and, stuffing Crump's mouth with Sen-Sen and his hands with dollars, he told the man to sober up, go away, and stay away. Watching all this, Marjoe was bewildered. How could a man who preached the gospel fall into such chronic sin?

But shortly after this, Crump discovered that although he was often too drunk to stand, he could still do a great job preaching sitting down. Somehow he financed a radio show, and began to make a little money. In evangelical circles it was said that God had blessed Crump with a radio ministry. God indeed had *so* blessed Crump that he was soon able to buy an expensive home in the best section of Fort Worth, where he installed his own broadcast studio. As long as he could see straight enough to get into his studio, his program went on the air daily, and he even began a crusade against alcohol and sermonized endlessly about his own salvation from the heinous stuff.

Thus, a few days after their departure from Cincinnati, the Gortners were hurrying toward the suburbs of Fort Worth. Marjoe noticed that Marge's intense scowling had stopped a day or so after they left Cincinnati, and this indicated to him that something new was in the process of developing. When they arrived he recognized O. B. Crump immediately—Crump was still a rotund man with a hearty laugh—but he was newly conscious, whenever he was within three feet of the man, of the pervasive odor of stale cigar smoke and gin.

His house reflected Brother Crump's sense of lavishness. (His wife had long since divorced him.) Every lamp and lighting fixture had crystal droplets or fringe, and in three of the rooms there was a completely stocked bar. Brother Crump's purple bedroom, its walls covered with gaudy paintings of nudes, was Marjoe's favorite, although he kept far away from it when his mother or Crump was in the house. Centered before a black velvet wall was an enormous bed, on either side of which stood two table lamps whose shades were decorated with nudes in provocative poses. When the lamps were turned on, the heat from the bulbs made the shades revolve, exposing various sections of the female anatomy. In the bathroom, next to the toilet, a stack of hard-core pornographic magazines was carefully arranged in a magazine rack. The master bedroom became Marjoe's hideaway.

What Marjoe found most interesting was his mother's reaction to Crump's lascivious kingdom. She feigned amusement, referring to Brother Crump as a "rascal," but beneath the giggling Marjoe could see that she was uncomfortable. He realized also that even though it was not an atmosphere she wanted her children exposed to, she would put up with it until they had the means to go somewhere else.

Every noon brought the chore of the radio broadcast. Brother Crump would bring a shaker of martinis and a box of cigars into the studio. Then, with a sly wink at Marjoe and Marge, he would begin his broadcast, slurping his martinis and puffing on his cigars, condemning the drunkards to hell and preaching the blood to those listeners addicted to the vice of tobacco. At midpoint in the broadcast Crump would motion for Marjoe to sit on his lap and address the radio audience. The Miracle Child was indestructibly famous in Texas, the passing years having had no effect on his reputation, and Marjoe's sermons during O. B. Crump's broadcasts were a boon to the radio ministry. His participation in the daily broadcast paid for the family's room and board.

In the hope of discovering a way out, Marge telephoned every evangelist she knew. She scoured the religion pages of the local papers. Even before Vernon left, Marjoe had been drawing smaller and smaller audiences, and the likelihood of returning to the gospel circuit without her husband's promotional efforts was bleak. But one day she found a quarter-page advertisement announcing that none other than the famous Jesse Kirkwood would be conducting a miracle restoration crusade five miles outside of town.

Marjoe's thirteenth birthday approached and his mother asked him what he wanted as a gift. He truthfully told her he would prefer one of Brother Crump's revolving lamps to any other present she could find. Much to his surprise, Marge learned where one could be bought and presented it to the boy on his birthday. He treasured his luminescent sexual merry-go-round, not so much for its charms but as evidence of his mother's continuing recognition of his maturity.

O. B. Crump, in the meantime, never allowed an occasion to pass without some mention of his genital endowment. After not many weeks the figure of twelve inches became standard. Furthermore, he had seen to it that this fact (if fact it was) should be immortalized photographically. These self-portraits were commonly mailed to his ex-wife, but he also took to leaving them around the bedroom. Inevitably the children saw them—Marjoe with little interest—and Marge felt that even for O. B. this went beyond any possible concept of acceptable behavior. She impatiently awaited Jesse Kirkwood's arrival in Texas.

A five-pole tent can seat about two thousand people, and

pitched on an open field on a blustery January day Marge found Kirkwood's portable canvas meeting hall surrounded with hundreds of automobiles. Marge circled the tent in the Buick, the children in the back seat, the luggage in the trunk, and Marjoe's revolving lamp under his arm. The meeting was scheduled to begin in fifteen minutes.

The interior of the tent was lighted by large quartz lamps powered by a portable generator located in a truck parked a hundred feet away. A portable runway with railings stood before a slightly raised platform. Onstage a five-piece gospel band played, and in the middle of the platform stood a huge white pulpit with a glistening gold cross. A wide banner above the stage announced CHRIST THE LIGHT.

Appearing with dramatic suddenness, Jesse Kirkwood strode to the pulpit dressed in celestial white. His voice roared out over the speakers around the tent, still corn-pone, but demanding and inspiring.

"Let's have church!" Kirkwood's fist thumped his pulpit.

"Let's have Jesus!

"Let's send the devil straight to Hell!

"Let's feel Jesus in our body!

"Let's love Jesus! Love him, *love him!*

"Are ya lonely? He's your friend!

"Hallelujah!

"Are ya scared? He's your comfort!

"Hallelujah!

"Are ya a sinner? He's Salvation!

"Hallelujah! Hallelujah! Praise the Lord!"

The roar in the tent was deafening.

"I said, I said, *praise him!* Praise him! I said we're here to praise the *Lord!*"

A member of Kirkwood's entourage had spotted the Gortners, and beckoned them up to seats on the back of the platform. Starloe looked puzzled as she whispered to Marjoe, "Why are we back *here?*"

"This is someone else's meeting. We're here to watch," he told her, and kissed her cheek. She gave him a lopsided six-year-old smile, half her baby teeth missing. The Gortners sat back in their seats and watched the crippled stumble forward to Kirkwood. The wheelchairs rolled up the runway. The arthritics and the hard of hearing wandered up. Women stood in their seats and babbled in tongues. When Kirkwood laid his hands on the sick they fell backward to the ground, shuddering, their eyes closed, their pockets emptied of their bills, twenty-dollar bills, tens, singles, Kirkwood bellowing and healing until the last coins tinkled into the buckets at the front of his platform. In a flash he disappeared as he had appeared. *That* was Kirkwood's church.

An hour later Marge Gortner and family were having steak dinner with Jesse Kirkwood.

"So young Marjoe here wants to team up with the Kirkwoods?" he said, chewing his meat. Marge gave him a convincing smile. Kirkwood studied the thirteen-year-old boy.

"Well . . . maybe for a few meetin's, anyway."

Jesse Kirkwood used the Gortners for several meetings, and Marjoe enjoyed preaching a few short sermons before Jesse took over the stage. But Kirkwood really didn't need him and no man in his position wanted to be burdened with three children. Marge Gortner, yes; not many men would be uninterested in Marge. But Marge herself knew that she needed a husband and father, not a lover.

Marge, in fact, was beginning to resign herself to the most desperate of all truths: she needed Vernon Gortner. In time she would have to tuck her pride away with her aspirations and find the man she had started out with.

The time came suddenly. Kirkwood cut short his stay in Fort Worth, having wrung every cent from the parishioners of the sponsoring church, and he headed on alone. Marge prepared the children for a reunion with their father. After several phone calls she had learned that Vernon actually had returned to his parents' home in Oakland, California. He had also, suddenly and mysteriously, become a vice-president of United States Industries, manufacturers of stainless steel products, and he owned a large amount of stock in the company. This apparent evidence of a nest egg infuriated Marge.

On the trip to Oakland, Marjoe felt sure that everything would work out once the family was back together. When they arrived they saw the familiar panel truck parked in front of the elder Gortners' home. But they were not invited in. Twenty feet away from the house stood a concrete storage building that Vernon had converted into an office. He explained that he had set up four cots on the cement floor for his wife and children. Also, his story remained the same. He had left them so *very* quickly because his mother *was* ill. He was sorry he hadn't time to say good-bye, but his mother had been on her deathbed.

"Is she dead?" Marge asked bluntly.

Vernon shook his head.

"No. The good lady's still hanging on. But the children in the house would be too much for her. This guest room will be comfortable enough."

Marge sent the children to the concrete bunker to unpack.

"What are you really here for, Marge?"

Marge buried her pride deep within her, along with her anger.

"A reconciliation. The children need you . . . I need you."

"And Dr. Miller. How is your friend Dr. Miller? I suppose he doesn't need you?"

Marge turned brusquely and walked into the bunker to help the children unpack.

Grandmother Gortner died a few months later, and Marjoe never found out whether or not Vernon needed onions to cry at her funeral. Clearly, no reconciliation was going to happen overnight. Vernon suggested that Marge find her own place to live; he would support her in the interim; and perhaps they could learn to trust and love each other again. Vernon never changed his tune. He'd look at Marge wistfully and say, "I never loved a woman more."

It was March before the family got together again.

Somewhere, somehow, Marge found an ex-airline pilot with only one arm who had a small house for rent in Big Sur, a few hundred miles from Oakland.

Vernon drove the family down to the Big Sur house. The

children were overjoyed. There was forest, mountains to hike in, the sea rushing toward the base of the cliffs below. Marge took Vernon and Marjoe to a small trading post on Route 1 and bought each boy a bow and arrow. Starloe got another doll to add to her small collection. Marjoe felt refreshed, relaxed. On weekdays he and Vernoe disappeared into the mysterious countryside for long, happy explorations. Early Friday afternoons Vernon appeared in the panel truck and spent the weekend with his family, and Saturdays the retired evangelists drove deeper into the mountains of Big Sur. Marjoe and Vernoe rushed through the forest shooting their arrows. The thirteen-year-old minister hadn't heard a "Glory!" or "Hallelujah!" in months and began finally to learn what peace was like. A full-time mother in her house and a part-time father on weekends was the happiest family situation they had thus far achieved.

But they had been in Big Sur only six weeks when this winter idyll ended. Marjoe and Vernoe had been darting around the trees when they noticed Marge and Vernon doing the same. Joyously they began to follow their parents through the forest until Marjoe detected a derisive note in Marge's voice as she called to Vernon. Finally Marjoe saw her only a few feet off. She was holding a handwritten paper and reading aloud from it in a sneering tone.

"That's a personal letter from Beth and you have no business . . ." Vernon shouted. Beth was Vernon's oldest daughter from his first marriage. Apparently, while he had been playing bows-and-arrows with the children in the woodland, Marge had been rummaging through his papers in the panel truck.

91

Eventually husband and wife collided, and Vernon was able to retrieve the letter. He ripped it to pieces. Then he piled them all back into the panel truck, dumped them at their house, and drove off.

Without Vernon to pay the rent, which was already two weeks behind, the one-armed pilot urged Marge to be on her way. She packed up the children and vacated the house. They traveled farther down the scenic coastline and arrived in Monterey.

Once again Marge rented a small house, opposite the Monterey Golf Course, and with what little money was left she tried to set up a comfortable home, with odds and ends of Salvation Army furniture and new curtains. Marjoe, deeply disturbed by the collapse of the Big Sur household, wanted positive reassurance that this would be their permanent place. In a grand gesture of affirmation that *this* house was to endure, Marge bought her son his first dog, a Great Dane. He was to be the symbol of her resolution to stabilize their lives. This symbol was named Gabriel, after the angel.

Much to Marjoe's surprise, Vernon paid an unscheduled visit to the Monterey house one weekend. His purpose was to announce that he was disgusted with it all. He told Marge he had no interest in trying anymore. It was over. Marge knew better than to plead with him. Offering no excuses to the children for breaking her latest promise, she sold Gabriel to a neighbor and the next week they trekked back to Oakland. There they checked into a hotel.

During the three miserable months that followed it turned out that the monthly payments on the still new Buick Roadmaster had not been made since November. It was not too surprising when two men from the General Motors Finance Corporation arrived at the hotel and repossessed the automobile. Vernon allowed them to take it, claiming that it was no longer his responsibility. He moved Marge and the children from the hotel into a small house nearby, where they stayed without a car, wholly dependent on his mercy. Finally, with no advance warning, Vernon bought them an old pink and black Ford convertible; it was his "settlement." Marge packed to leave. They were going back on the road.

Marjoe by then was reduced to sullen resignation and resentment. He shrugged when Marge told him her decision—next stop, Seattle, Washington. She called on an old friend from her Canadian Sisters days to set up a meeting to get them started. Marjoe ran through his list of sermons, and chose what had been a sure-fire congregation-rouser. At the meeting Vernoe sang a short song and then Marjoe tried to fire the congregation into emptying their wallets. A bit rusty, and more than a bit bored, he generated only a medium take. Undaunted, Marge booked another meeting, one in which she had a special interest.

Vancouver, Washington, was the home of a minister Marge had met several times during her evangelical wanderings. But so far time and circumstance had not provided the chance for them to get to know each other better. Paris Simon Coolidge was the eclectic name of the pious man who had graciously offered the family their next meeting. Coolidge was exceptionally hospitable. He invited them to Vancouver for a two-week stint, and he even paid for advertising from his own budget.

His church, though not as large as many that the Gortners had appeared in, was popular and well respected.

Coolidge reserved two rooms for the family at the finest hotel in the city. He greeted Marge and the family like visiting diplomats and this deferential treatment immediately reactivated Marge. Opening night she donned one of her famous tapered white suits. Her eyes sparkled at Coolidge and dimmed coolly in the presence of his wife. Arriving at the packed church just before the meeting began, she insisted that Marjoe preach "Hell with the Lid Off." If things went as well as expected, she even considered doing "From Wheelchair to Pulpit" the following week.

The meeting went off better than Marge had hoped, just like the good old days. Marjoe was able to throw in a few high-pressure gimmicks he had learned from Jesse Kirkwood, and the money poured in.

The evening of their last meeting, Coolidge had dinner with the family. Marge was in excellent humor, the younger children were happy, and even though Marjoe was not overjoyed at being the family breadwinner again, the evening had been triumphant enough to raise his spirits.

The three youngsters were brought back to their hotel. As they prepared for bed, Marjoe noticed that Mom-Marge didn't seem on the verge of retiring.

"Aren't you going to sleep?" he asked.

"No . . ." She paused, probably deciding whether she should level with the boy.

Finally, "I have some business to discuss with Brother Coolidge."

94

Marge hurried downstairs and got into Paris Coolidge's waiting car. They drove through downtown Vancouver, heading for a less populous area nearby. As they stopped at a traffic light, the three men in the car behind them recognized their minister's automobile. It was ordinary enough to see Brother Coolidge and his wife driving through the city, but Mrs. Coolidge was a brunette. The woman with the minister was blond.

Unaware that they were being followed, Coolidge and Marge drove six miles out of town to a two-story motel and got out of the car. The three parishioners immediately recognized the white-suited blonde as Sister Gortner. Allowing the pair to check in, they watched them climb a stairway, pass the second-floor balcony, and enter a room. Then the three had a long discussion with the desk clerk, and finally rented the adjoining room.

Within an hour the most prominent members of Coolidge's congregation were assembled with their wives in the parking lot below. Several men remained in the adjoining room with their ears pressed against the wall. Three hours later Marge and Coolidge emerged.

Below stood some twenty-odd people. On either side of the doorway members of the congregation flanked their minister and the visiting evangelist. Coolidge blanched. His hand trembled as he stepped away from his paramour. Marge's eyes widened as she took in the crowd below. Her back stiffened, her lips pursed, and she strode to the railing as if ascending a pulpit. Then she addressed the waiting audience in a distinct, dignified voice.

"Brother Coolidge and I . . . have just had a wonderful prayer meeting."

All these years Marjoe had wondered what it would be like to be run out of town, but when it happened he didn't even know it. There was no tarring and feathering. Marge's behavior continued to be dignified and reserved. Their meetings were over, and they would move on, this time to Los Angeles.

In the dark night that followed, Marjoe sat by his mother's side as she drove down Route 1, past Oakland, Big Sur, Santa Cruz.

"Maybe we can get in another good meeting in Los Angeles," she told Marjoe.

"Who with?"

"Remember Bonnerz at Emmanuel Tabernacle?"

"That's small-time," Marjoe told her.

"Not anymore. The church has been rebuilt and enlarged. He has a monthly newsletter and he's got a pretty good business manager too."

In Los Angeles, Bruce Benjamin, Bonnerz's business manager, met them at the Emmanuel Tabernacle and accompanied them to the Los Angeles Hilton. Marge parked the pink and black convertible in the parking lot while Benjamin checked them in. Benjamin affected highly styled iridescent suits and wing-tip shoes; his hair was slicked back and he had a tiny mustache. Before they had even unpacked Marjoe knew that Benjamin was a likely candidate for Marge's next helping hand.

The following day they met with Oliver Bonnerz and toured

his newly built church. Benjamin trailed behind, pointing out minute details of the architecture.

"Bruce is an excellent businessman," Bonnerz confided to Marge. "He's a great producer."

A week later the pink and black Ford convertible was missing from the Hilton parking lot. Marge telephoned Vernon in Oakland; the registration had again been in his name. Vernon had decided not to make the payments on this car either. If he and Marge were not together, why should he pay for her transportation? Wild with frustration, Marge told him on the phone that she would start divorce proceedings to force him to support her and the children. Under California State law, half of everything Vernon owned would soon be hers.

It was nearly a year since Vernon had first left them. Wandering through the country in the old days had been tiresome for Marjoe, but at least it had been purposeful. Now they wandered out of desperation. It disturbed him to be preaching in Bonnerz's church, and he was conscious that in the background Marge and Benjamin were cooking up some scheme. It took only a week for them to unveil it. Benjamin gave Marjoe a dazzling prophecy of the months to come.

"Listen, kid: Marjoe Returns! A small man but a giant-killer against juvenile delinquency!" His hand punctuated the sentences in the air, as though spelling them out on a marquee.

"We did that already," Marjoe told him.

"This'll be different. I'm telling you! Leave it to old Bruce."

Marjoe left nothing to anyone. It was he who planned what he would do every day during his booking in Bonnerz's church. And it was he who suffered the "Glories" and the "Hal-

lelujahs" like salt in an open wound. The repetition, the *endless*
repetition . . . The night of his last scheduled meeting finally
arrived. The family was due to check out of the Hilton and into
Bruce Benjamin's apartment the next day.

Marge was standing behind Starloe, putting some finishing
touches on her blond hair, when Marjoe led her into the next
room and seated her in a green-and-salmon-printed chair. He
looked intently at her for a long time. Then he smiled. He
spoke to her like a young man in total control of his life.

"This is my last sermon, Mother. I'm quitting the business."

"Don't be ridiculous, Marjoe. What would you do?"

"I'd be a normal thirteen-year-old boy."

"You're thirteen anyway, and God gave you a ministry. You
have a responsibility—"

"I'm quitting the business. This is my last sermon." Then
he turned and walked to the door, while Marge burst into tears.

Shutting the hotel door behind him, Marjoe found his way
alone to Bonnerz's church. That night he chalked up one more
blow for the Almighty, one more cut in the percentage of the
take, and he stood firm in his decision.

"What if I get you booked into the Masonic Temple? Eh?
The largest in L.A.!" Benjamin asked him the next day. Marjoe
shook his head. He spent the day walking along Hollywood
Boulevard, studying the people, the stores, thinking about the
blank future.

That evening, over dinner, Benjamin disconcertedly told the
family he had been unable to book the Masonic Temple.

"But all we need is a gimmick. We'll be right back up there, in the big time again." He glared at Marjoe, stubborn in his silence. "How'd you like your own church, kid?"

Marge brightened at the prospect. Marjoe remained deliberately uncommunicative. Benjamin aimed his optimistic rhetoric at Marge.

"If the kid's not interested we've gotta find another gimmick. What about little Vernoe here?" He reached toward the boy. Vernoe ducked, flinching in pain; a threatened ulcer was just beginning to heal. Marge shook her head no. Another long silence. Then, slowly, all heads turned toward Starloe.

Starloe Gortner was dressed in a white party dress, four crinolines showing below the hem. The famous blond hair was pulled back, tiny white gloves covered her hands, white socks fell at her ankles. Sunday, November 17, 1957, she was photographed for the *Los Angeles Examiner* with an open Bible in her hand and a toothless mouth spouting the gospel. The entire story follows:

Child Evangelist, 7, Climbs Pulpit Today

Seven year old evangelist Starloe Gortner today will begin her personal "worldwide youth-to-youth campaign against juvenile delinquency" with a sermon at the Embassy Auditorium.

At 2:30 p.m. she will take the pulpit as a minister.

Although seven may seem an early age to begin a preaching career, Starloe is the "late starter" of her family.

Her brother, Marjoe, now 13, was only four years old when he became a minister. Another brother, Vernoe, also is a minister.

Their mother, the Rev. Marge Gortner, herself an evangelist, said Starloe has been helping with the musical portions of her brothers' services since she was three, but only recently became interested in preaching.

"She used to hide in the closet," said the Rev. Mrs. Gortner, "and preach to her dolls, or to an empty room or to the backyard. Sometimes I would hear her, but she would never ask to preach in public, so I waited.

DEDICATED LIVES

"Now, however, she has asked to preach, and we know that she can preach, and so that is what she will do."

The Rev. Gortner and her three children have pledged their lives, they said, to a fight against juvenile delinquency.

"We feel," she said, "that children can speak best to other children, and that is why Marjoe, Vernoe and Starloe have been chosen to carry the word around the world.

"We will visit many towns in California and then go to the South Seas, to Australia and to other places around the world where children are in need of help."

It was Marge's last meeting. Benjamin tried to book Starloe into local churches, but failed. Starloe just didn't have any preaching talent, and the new deals and gimmicks all fell through. Marge began to call him "Bruce Who Could Not Produce."

For a while the family lived in a series of depressing hotels along Hollywood Boulevard. When the rent came due they would move out in the middle of the night. Marjoe became expert at quick packing and shifting. He understood and sympathized with his mother's situation, but Marge herself refused to spend time or energy bemoaning their fallen state. She had to get the family moving again.

One day she returned to the dumpy hostelry they were holed

up in, looking like someone who had been handed a present.

"Pots and pans and kettles and cans!" she said to Marjoe. "I've met a wonderful fellow who's district manager of a housewares concern. He's driving us up to Palo Alto and I'm going to start selling."

The children brightened at the prospect of Palo Alto, the country, and the forest. The "pots and pans, kettles and cans" district manager was an amiable fellow named Joe Green and on the way to Palo Alto Marge revealed the special surprise in store for her children. They were going to live on a ranch.

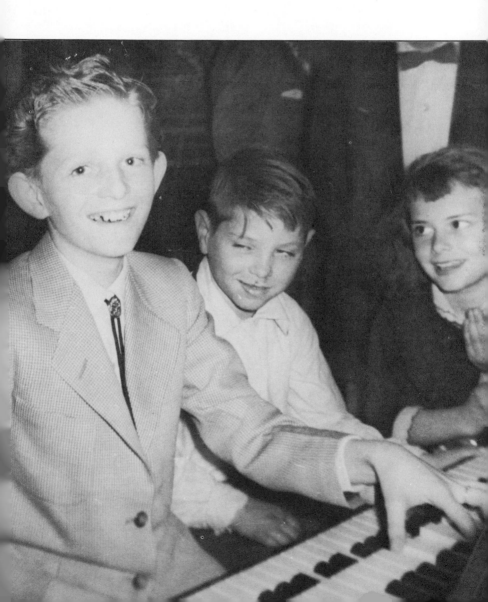

CHAPTER 5

 The Rocking Horse Ranch was paradise. And even more wonderful was Frances Kaler, its proprietor. Franny, as she insisted the children call her, was only five feet tall, a fifty-year-old, rough-and-ready, Annie Get Your Gun woman, whose dust-colored cowboy boots added a scant two inches to her height. At her first meeting with Marge the contrast between the two was almost ludicrous. As they chatted, Marge loomed over her, the acme of respectability, neat dress, modish hair, silver courtesy. Finally Frances wiped her hands on the back of her blue jeans and gave Marge a big smile. Further wrinkling up a very wrinkled face, she said wryly, "I know us two are gonna be great pals."

Marjoe fell for Franny at first sight. Hopalong Cassidy for a mother—that's who she was! Franny looked over Starloe in her prissy dress. "Gotta get you some fittin' clothes," she told her. Then she grabbed Vernoe gently by the ear. "Ever seen some goats, Vern?"

"Sure!" Vernoe gave her a cherubic smile.

"Well, you'll see some more down back of the barn."

Vernoe paused, looking expectantly at his mother.

"Gowan," Franny told him. "See yourself some more."

"And you," she said roughly to Marjoe, who stood beside her, gangly and all smiles. "Ever do any riding?"

"Yes," he told her, and then couldn't resist bragging. "I even rode an elephant once." This stumped Franny.

"Well, we ain't got no elephants here, but we've got horses."

By the next morning Franny had the three children outfitted in proper western clothes. Marjoe followed her around the ranch. Four hundred feet from the main house stood a large kennel with a metal-gated running area. Ten or fifteen German shepherd puppies bounded up to the fence.

"What do you do with all of them?" Marjoe asked.

"I breed 'em. Some of the finest bitches in the West here at Rockin' Horse. You like dogs?"

"Sure!" Marjoe told her eagerly. "We had two chihuahuas, Bambi and Blueboe, and some pink poodles my mom used to breed, and my last one"—Marjoe thought back wistfully to the broken promises of Monterey—"was a Great Dane named Gabriel."

"Interesting names," Frances Kaler said thoughtfully, kicking the earth around in front of the kennel.

"Your mother's got a knack for interesting names." She paused again and stuck her nose through the wire fence. Immediately five puppies licked her face. "What's your *real* name, son?"

"*Marjoe,*" he answered. Frances let it drop.

105

"The father of six of these's called Champion Rexforth Hollofield," she told the boy a few minutes later. "That's a *real* name."

They crossed back past the house. Marge was about to leave with Joe Green on her first pot-and-pan-selling trip. She warned Marjoe to behave himself and to take care of his brother and sister until she got back in the late afternoon.

"Your mom and dad are ministers, huh?" Franny asked the boy.

"Yes, ma'am." Marjoe's instinct warned him against boasting about his own anointing.

Vernoe was already up at the stables, stumbling through the manure and hay. Patiently Franny introduced the boys to the horses there, and left them tending a mare while she went off to look after her other chores.

Frances Kaler studied Marge's every move. She watched Joe Green pick her up in the morning and return her in time for dinner with the children. She watched as Green began to return after dinner and take Marge out for the evening. She watched as other salesmen called for Marge in new convertibles. She watched a man named Roland Hunter bring flowers for Marge and gifts for the children. She watched Marge drag herself home after a hard day selling pots and pans and perk up rapidly as she dressed for her evening date. For many weeks she watched in silence, as the feeling grew that the children were more hers than their mother's.

One weekend Marge disappeared with Roland Hunter, promising to return the next day with a special surprise for

Marjoe. They came back to Rocking Horse Ranch on Sunday, Roland's car towing a huge trailer. Marjoe spotted them from the pasture and raced to meet them, reaching the trailer in time to see them unloading a full-size black and white pinto pony. Marjoe stood rooted to the ground as Starloe and Vernoe straggled up alongside him, and he was wordless as Roland handed him the reins. All the horses he had ridden in the past belonged to someone else, often to lucky children who had home lives and possessions they could keep. Now he held the reins of his own pony, and he was filled with the sweetest happiness he could imagine.

"It's yours!" Marge said.

Involuntarily Frances Kaler hugged Marjoe. Her embrace released him from his trance, and he ran up to the pony and petted its nose.

"Whatcha gonna call him?" Frances asked.

"Comanche! My own horse! Comanche!"

How Marge and Roland had wangled a pony for her son was just another unaccountable entry in the long list of Marge's miracles. Indisputably, it was Marjoe's favorite. Leading Comanche by the reins, he strode to the stables beside Frances, and together they maneuvered the new pony into a stall. Then Marjoe set about grooming and feeding his treasure, under Franny's watchful eye. There was no need for her to explain that Comanche was to be totally Marjoe's responsibility. Everything about the horse was a joy: training, grooming, shoeing. Franny would show him how, but it would be Marjoe's job.

Marge made arrangements to hit Vernon with her long postponed demand for a divorce. Joe Green drove her to the Oakland house where her husband was waiting.

Their initial cordiality was short-lived, and Marge got down to business. She wanted alimony and, naturally, support for her three children.

"You think you're mother to those three children, don't you?" Vernon asked her.

"So we *say*," Marge answered sardonically.

Vernon puttered around the room for a while, then turned to Marge. He was at his most charming.

"You know, I was offered a ministry three weeks ago," he said.

What was this? Marge sat upright. Another conciliatory gesture coming?

"Oh, really? Oh, nice." She paused a long time. So did Vernon. "Where?" she finally asked.

"Vancouver. Paris Simon Coolidge was asked to leave his church." Vernon was telling the truth. He had indeed been offered the church.

Marge inhaled, exhaled, then inhaled again. Vernon continued. "Seems he ran into a little trouble up there with some woman evangelist. Never was a place in evangelism for women, the Bible said."

"Don't you quote the Bible to me!" Marge shouted.

"And the California laws," Vernon outshouted her, "say there's enough evidence in this case to prove a woman an unfit mother. Take her children right away from her!"

Marge left.

Early mornings Marjoe attended to Comanche's grooming in the stable. Except for distant animal noises, it was usually very quiet. But this morning there was a strange shaking sound in Comanche's stall. Rattlesnake! Marjoe jumped over the sideboard and grabbed a pitchfork. He thought of leading Comanche out of the stall but he was afraid of any sudden movement. Hanging over the edge of the next stall, he saw the rattler slide its way toward Comanche's right leg. Marjoe stopped breathing. He raised the pitchfork high over his head and plunged it toward the snake. Missed! The rattler reared back angrily. Taking careful aim, Marjoe plunged the fork down again, this time catching the snake squarely behind its head. He watched it writhe in agony, venom spurting through its hollow fangs, only inches from where Comanche stood. In a moment it was dead.

Frances was overjoyed at Marjoe's heroism. She taught him how to flay the snake and salt the skin. In a week he had it nailed to a board that hung over his bed.

From then on Marjoe regarded himself as Franny's right-hand man, and she encouraged him in this conviction. When the local kennel club sponsored a dog show, she asked him to be her principal assistant.

"Lots of responsibility, this. Think you can handle it?"

"Promise," he said.

Frances started him on a daily schedule. After each meal Marjoe would cut the fat from leftover meat and feed it to Champion Rexforth Hollofield. Frances taught Marjoe to show the dog, walking him in a wide oval, keeping the leash high. He brushed Rexforth with the same determination he displayed in grooming Comanche. He held the dog's muzzle while Frances brushed its teeth. He marked off the days on the calendar in his room, and on the morning of the show he woke at dawn and brushed the dog for an extra hour.

Rexforth was allowed to sit in the front seat of the pickup truck on the way to the show, while Marjoe sat in the open wagon, beaming with pride as they drove along the highway.

Champion Rexforth Hollofield wasn't even a finalist at the show. After the judging was over, Frances went to collect the dog from its cage behind the show area. Marjoe was standing ten feet away, looking as if he were about to cry.

"You're not poutin', are you?" she shouted to him.

"No," he said, trying to stop.

"Good thing. My ranch hands can't go around poutin'. Especially when we were so damn good. Just the judges who didn't think so."

And she cursed them all the way home.

Not many weeks later Marge learned that Vernon meant what he had threatened: no alimony or he would take the children. And Franny Kaler decided to have a talk with Marge. The two women had successfully avoided having anything to do with each other on a personal basis. Marge was on time with her rent money, but Franny could no longer shrug off the fact that socially and morally she found Marge in arrears.

She put up a pot of strong black coffee and squared off to talk with Marge in her little kitchen. They sat facing one another like strangers seated at the same restaurant table.

"You're an attractive woman," Franny said.

Marge did not automatically consider this a compliment. She took a sip of coffee and nodded. Kaler was up to something.

"You've got a lot of men friends," Franny went on.

"That's no concern of yours, Mrs. Kaler."

"Maybe not. But the problem is so *many* men friends. I take it Mr. Green knows nothing about Mr. Hunter?"

Marge nodded again.

"I don't condemn a woman for wanting to live her life. I'm sure you're a good woman. A minister and all. But the kids ain't gettin' their fair shakes."

Marge stood up, pushing away from the table, infuriated at this old tomboy's impudence.

"Mrs. Kaler, my personal life has nothing—"

"The court would take them kids away from you, you know. I could give them a home. They'd get—"

But Marge had already raced from the kitchen.

A two-door sedan. Gray with a black interior. Six years old. Forty-three thousand miles on the odometer. The suitcases were in the trunk. Vernoe and Starloe waited outside. Marjoe was down at the stable, saying good-bye to Comanche. He met Franny halfway up the path toward the car. He began to speak but she stopped him.

"No such things as good-byes," she said firmly. Then she pulled affectionately at his hair. "See ya around, cowboy."

Marjoe walked rigidly to the car, dazed, torn, his eyes misted. He watched Marge intently as she started the car and they drove away, and he vowed he would never mention

111

Frances Kaler's name again. Franny stood on the dirt road, watching them leave. Hours after the car was out of sight, she was still at the stables grooming Comanche.

In 1952, when Marjoe was eight years old, a woman named Dolores Hopkins had given a tiny diamond ring to the Miracle Child after hearing him preach in Coldwater, Michigan. The ring was a family heirloom, last worn by her only child, Sonny, when he was a small boy. Eight years after Sonny had been reported missing in action on the Russian front, she gave Marjoe the ring in gratitude for the religious solace he had brought her. Dolores Hopkins was a patient woman of very modest intelligence. She had promised the Gortner family that if they were ever in need, her small farm in Coldwater was available to them for refuge.

Need there was. Marge had done many harsh things to her children, but she loved them, and in the end they would always be hers. All the laws of the state of California, all the Frances Kalers, all of Vernon's threats would not get those children away from her.

The ring that Dolores Hopkins had given Marjoe was the last object Marge had pawned. When they arrived at the Hopkins farm in Michigan there was too much excitement and confusion for it to be remembered at all. The despaired-of Sonny, after spending a year in a prisoner-of-war camp and thirteen years in the psychiatric ward of a veterans' hospital in Virginia, had recently remembered who he was and returned to his mother's house in Coldwater to live out his shattered life. But in the interim Mrs. Hopkins had fared little better. She had herself suffered a nervous collapse in 1954, and when the Gortners arrived at the Hopkins farm in 1958 it was far from an ideal refuge.

The loss of Frances Kaler and Comanche was a paralyzing blow to Marjoe, and he was still numb. Vernoe, internalizing his feelings as always, remained neutral about the move, and to Starloe the new house was just part of the continuing adventure. But Marge was horrified at what they found. Sonny lurched through the house all day, and she was awakened their first night by a hideous screeching from the living room. Trembling, she unlocked her bedroom door and tiptoed downstairs to discover Sonny in the act of slaughtering a chicken. Feathers were settling everywhere.

"No *no!*" Mrs. Hopkins was saying patiently to Sonny. "No more chickens in the house."

Sonny's vacant eyes stared down at the butchered bird. In his right hand he held a large knife gummy with blood. Marge sucked in her cheeks and hurried back upstairs, on the edge of panic as she locked her door.

The next night brought more of the same: squawking, screeching, feathers, blood, and the knife. Once again Marge listened from the bottom of the stairs as Mrs. Hopkins tried to explain to Sonny.

"We don't need any more chickens, Sonny. We've got enough chickens to last *two weeks!* Please, Sonny, no more chickens!"

At the end of their first week Marge embraced Mrs. Hopkins warmly, assuring her that she and Sonny would never be forgotten, and fled the farm with her children intact.

113

In planning her flight from the Hopkins farm Marge had made some long-distance calls to her father in Dallas, Texas. Her stepmother, Nellie, had died and now Stuart McMillan had hired a woman to manage the tiny antique shop he had bought with his wife's insurance money. The new manageress was very reluctant to call Stuart McMillan to the phone, and Marge was soon fuming at this unwarranted interference between father and daughter. When she finally succeeded in getting through to her father she was apprehensive as well as angry. Challenged, Stuart McMillan grudgingly admitted that he had been thinking of turning the shop over to the manageress.

"Don't do a thing till I get there!" Marge warned him.

The trip to Texas from Michigan took longer than Marge intended. The old two-door sedan kept breaking down, and by the time they reached Dallas they were broke again.

They arrived to discover that the Reverend McMillan had been so well befriended by the manageress that he had given her a free hand in financial matters. Marge immediately offered to run the shop herself.

"And give up your ministry?" McMillan innocently asked.

"Yes. We'll settle here with you. It'll be very nice. In the meanwhile, *don't sell that store!*"

Stuart McMillan owned an old station wagon that was sufficient transportation around Dallas, but Marjoe wanted the family to have their own car. The sedan had to be junked.

Marjoe was fourteen, tall enough and experienced enough to drive although according to the law he was too young. For his own reasons, he was eager for his mother to have her own car.

Marge made a deal with him.

"Suppose we call up Tucker Jamieson."

"Jamieson! That fat fairy?" Marjoe asked.

"Oh, I think we can handle him now, and with a couple of good meetings, we can get a new car."

Marjoe thought it over. It was a deal. He'd preach for a car.

Tucker was glad to see Marjoe again. "But you've grown up so!" he told him. "Really, such an impressive young man. I'm at a loss . . ."

Good, Marjoe thought. Stay that way.

"Now, where are all of you living?"

"With my father," Marge said.

"Yes, of course. And how is he?" Jamieson asked.

"Well, he hasn't been—"

"I know what!" Tucker interrupted. "You remember Artie, don't you?" Marge nodded. Tucker turned to Marjoe. "Remember Artie, dear?" Marjoe nodded too.

"Well, I bought him that cute little building he was living in. And—surprise! There's an empty apartment! You can move right in! How's that? Tucker takes care of his people! Right, dear?" He fluttered his handkerchief at them and lifted his enormous weight from his chair.

"All settled then?" he demanded.

Marge looked at Marjoe and he shrugged hopelessly. The

115

little house Stuart McMillan lived in was too small for them anyway. They might as well allow themselves to be shuttled into Artie's building.

Jamieson's congregation had increased in size since Marjoe had last preached there, but most of the parishioners still remembered Marjoe and the family, and the two-week stint was pleasant and profitable. They made enough money for a new car and began searching for a house of their own. Marge clung to the hope of taking over the McMillan antique shop. "And after all," as she told Marjoe, "Dallas really isn't a bad place to live."

The following week Marge made appointments for her sons to take entrance examinations at Sacred Heart. An expensive parochial school, Sacred Heart offered both a sensible educational program and the sort of students Marge wanted her sons to associate with. Marjoe's exam score placed him in the ninth grade, along with his age group. Vernoe was placed a year behind the other eleven-year-olds. That accomplished, Marge rented a comfortable house in walking distance of McMillan Antiques.

After a week at Sacred Heart, Marjoe realized that the student body did not correspond very closely to the description in the school brochure. His classmates were mostly children of rich Dallasites who found the school a convenient place to discipline and tone down offspring they could not themselves control. One such was Marjoe's first friend, Leonard Starker.

Although he was sixteen years old, Starker was still in the ninth grade. He was the school bully. The fathers of other Sacred Heart students were prominent men in Texas and the southwest, congressmen and bankers and doctors. But Starker's father was a nationally famous wrestler, in other words, in show business, and a brute. Starker was hated at Sacred Heart.

When Marjoe and Starker first met, there was an instinctive empathy between them. It hadn't taken long for word to circulate in study hall and lunchroom that Marjoe was a minister, and a famous one at that. And although he was affable, and was careful not to brag, there was something—perhaps the long years without the companionship of other boys—which set him apart and drew him to the other "outsider."

At first Marjoe tried to convince Starker that there was no need to live up to his father's reputation, but he soon saw it was useless. Starker thrived on the negative respect he received from the other students, and because he was a sixteen-year-old surrounded by younger children, his role of bully was easy to play. And when things got too quiet, Starker would always find some way to enhance his reputation. But although Starker boasted loudly of his sexual accomplishments, Marjoe was sure he was a virgin. Marjoe, on the other hand, preaching one Sabbath at Jamieson's Sunday school, had discovered the Sunday school teacher, a wide-hipped young lady of twenty-one who found Marjoe much to her fancy. Since he saw no reason not to fancy back, they began a short-lived affair. Leaving Sunday school together, they would check into a motel and spend the day in bed.

Starker was totally incredulous when Marjoe told him what was happening, and his friendship with Marjoe took on the character of a sacred relationship in his eyes.

Starker's prized possession was a Winchester 30/30 rifle,

117

which he kept hidden under the back seat of the family car. When the Starker car was unavailable, and Marge was using the Gortners', the two boys cruised Dallas in Grandfather McMillan's station wagon. Friday nights every student in the school with a driver's license drove to the school parking lot to exchange dirty jokes and stories, and to fight. Leonard Starker was always the prime target of the fights, and he kept his Winchester in the back seat as psychological insurance.

Several Friday nights in a row Starker had a swing-out with one or two younger boys and the seniors at Sacred Heart decided on the Friday following that Starker was going to pay his dues. As soon as he and Marjoe arrived in the parking lot, Starker was surrounded by three of the seniors. Somebody pulled a car up in front of them, blocking the driveway, and fists started thumping on the windows, hard enough to break the glass.

Marjoe turned to Starker. "Get out and I'll turn the car around!"

Starker bravely entered the melee and threw a few punches while Marjoe backed the car around. By then two boys were holding Starker while two others were hitting him. Marjoe revved the engine and drove straight at the group. All they could see was the glare of the headlights and the automobile barreling toward them. The attackers scattered and Starker jumped on the hood of the car, holding onto the windshield wipers. Marjoe stopped the car thirty feet away and Starker got behind the steering wheel. They tore out of the side entrance to the parking lot and turned down a deserted street. Suddenly there were headlights behind them and another car racing straight at their rear. Starker stepped on the accelerator while Marjoe crawled into the back seat, panic-stricken, trying to find the Winchester.

By now both cars were doing sixty miles an hour down the Texas roads.

"I've got to lower this back window!" Marjoe called. He finally found the handle and the rear window of the station wagon retreated. Carefully aiming the 30/30, he blew two holes in the right front tire of the pursuing car. A half hour later Starker pulled up in front of the McMillan house. Neither boy had spoken after the shooting.

"Where'd you learn to do that?" Starker asked.

"In Cincinnati. With rats."

Marjoe said it as though it were no accomplishment at all.

All day Saturday Starker and Marjoe waited for the police to come and take them away, but nothing happened, their assailants having probably concluded that they had as much to lose as Starker and Marjoe. By Saturday night Starker was feeling cocky again and suggested another cruise around Dallas, promising to avoid the Sacred Heart parking lot.

He had, however, a penchant for parking lots. This time they wound up outside the city hospital. Starker pointed to a car twenty feet away.

"Pretty neat spinners, huh?"

The car was equipped with chrome spinner hub caps.

"They're beauties!" Marjoe told him.

"Let's take them," Starker suggested.

Marjoe was fascinated by the idea, but he was also afraid.

"I don't want to, Starker."

119

"They'd look really great on your mother's new car, Gortner. What would your Sunday school teacher think?"

"No. C'mon, let's get out of here."

"Reverend Marjoe," Starker taunted, "you're not scared, are you?"

"I won't do it, Lenny. Really, I won't."

"Then let me!" Starker demanded. Marjoe could not bring himself to get out of the car.

"Do what you want," he said.

Starker took a wrench from the trunk of the car and removed the rear right spinner. He was working on the front one when three men walked out of the darkness and pushed him up against the car. In seconds Marjoe was pulled outside and held next to Starker. Soon there were sirens and police. Marjoe gave Starker a dirty look, then stared at the ground all the way to the local precinct.

Surprisingly, Marge never reprimanded her son. Not in front of the police, nor at home. She left him to face his conscience and whatever burden of guilt he felt. Sacred Heart was less broad-minded. Leonard Starker and Marjoe were expelled the following day.

Marge continued to divide her time between her father and his shop. But Stuart McMillan, after what he referred to as "careful thought," decided to allow his manageress to move into his house. Marge bitterly acknowledged one more defeat and a dreary month passed during which Marjoe sulked around the house or went to see his girl. Marge seemed to be waiting again. When the Blackwoods passed through Dallas, she went to see Jesse alone. She came home depressed. He hadn't offered her a meeting, not even a one-nighter. There was no work available in town. Vernoe was doing poorly in school. Where were the Canadian Sisters? Where was stardom? Marge Gortner was forty-five years old. She had gained weight. Her hips had spread. Her eyes fogged as though from cataracts. She longed for the ocean and the mountains. She wanted to start all over again. She wanted to wave a wand and make it all disappear. She even prayed.

In 1960 she saw her father for the last time. She woke the children at sunrise. Marjoe had already packed the car. She drove for days, first to the shore of Southern California, then north past Long Beach and Laverne, past Los Angeles and Bonnerz and Bruce Benjamin. She stopped late one night in the honky-tonk resort of Santa Cruz, and the next day she found a ramshackle house, hidden between the redwoods and the ocean, the mountains and the gravel pits, in an empty town called Felton. For the first time in fifteen years she was going to stay put.

Vernon arrived a month later to retrieve Vernoe. Marge had pretended that the little boy was going off on a marvelous vacation with his daddy; Marjoe, knowing this was no temporary separation, felt envious of Vernoe for the first time. Vernoe watched with big eyes as his belongings were piled into the trunk of Vernon's car. Marge kissed him good-bye and began to weep, but Vernoe never flinched. He walked majestically to the car and did not look back.

121

The Reverend Marge Gortner was now plain Mrs. Gortner. The Reverend Marjoe Gortner was called Ross, which was his middle name. He made the adjustment with great relief. They pretended they were just plain folks, and within a week, head held high and spirits low, Marge put on a blue uniform and became the day-shift waitress of the greasy-spoon Felton Diner.

"Hey, Maggie," the fat truck drivers called to her. "What slop you dishing out today?" And she smiled at them, having traveled the thousands of miles, lived the hundreds of dreams, lost the countless chances of what seemed like so many life-times.

CHAPTER 6

The house in Felton had fourteen rooms and had not been lived in for six years. The last occupants had turned it into a boardinghouse in the late 1940s and each room on the second and third floors had a tiny number affixed to the door. Marge's first act of renovation was to remove the numbers and repaint the doors.

With her second week's salary she bought cheap curtains for the kitchen, her bedroom, and Marjoe's room. She collected the dimes and quarters from her tips in a mayonnaise jar that she kept in the kitchen. And every morning she woke up at seven to cook breakfast for Marjoe and Starloe and get to the diner by nine.

At night, when she came home tired and bedraggled after putting up all day with the taunts of the customers, she made dinner for her son and Starloe and went to bed early. Marjoe drove down into Santa Cruz each night and strolled the boardwalk with the tourists.

A month passed. Two. Three months. A divorce decree was mailed to her: divorced by Vernon Gortner on grounds of "incompatibility." No alimony or settlement. But "incompatibility" was Vernon's gesture of generosity.

In another month a man began to pick Marge up at the house in Felton. He was tall and had large, clumsy hands. Marjoe was introduced to him as Ross Gortner. Having a new friend seemed to cheer Marge a great deal, and Marjoe was happy for her.

The man's name was Carl Warner, and he had met Marge in the diner. As the weeks passed she began to talk more about him and also about the Felton Diner. Felton lay ten miles north of Santa Cruz, along the truck route from the huge sand and gravel pits farther up in the mountains which supplied most of the materials for the cement companies in Northern California. The busy route was also followed by eight-ton produce trucks, and Marge, even in her capacity as waitress, had made the acquaintance of several wealthy mine owners and some well-to-do produce wholesalers as well. Carl Warner was owner of the second largest gravel pit in the area. Marjoe didn't need to think twice about the outcome; he sensed Marge was not long for the Felton Diner.

Warner, indeed, had agreed to invest several thousand dollars in a new business for Marge. George Curtis, a man who owned a big vineyard, was to invest the additional capital needed. The situation, of course, held Marge's special brand of complexity; Carl Warner thought he was Marge's only benefactor, and she had persuaded George Curtis to believe the same thing. The result of all this was Marge's own diner along the main truck route. It was named Marge's Pit. A long way from "From Wheelchair to Pulpit."

124

At the grand opening of Marge's Pit, Curtis and Warner sat at opposite ends of the counter, grinning at each other, each holding four aces. Marjoe, now firmly established as Ross, was in the kitchen working at his new job: short-order cook.

Cook Ross Gortner was six feet tall and would soon reach his full six feet three inches. Dressed in white apron and chef's hat, he looked and felt somewhat out of place. He also knew right away that he didn't belong in the kitchen of Marge's Pit, and didn't want any part in Marge's own arrangements. He felt most at ease, naturally enough, in the carnival world of the Santa Cruz boardwalk.

The western coastline of Northern California is astonishingly beautiful. Forests run to the edge of towering cliffs; thousands of feet below, the Pacific Ocean comes rushing toward the land, forming dazzling inlets, coves, and storybook beaches. Seventy-three miles south of San Francisco, the city of Santa Cruz exists like a pimple of civilization in a noble wilderness, a layered community leading down to an inlet beach and a clump of boardwalk.

Santa Cruz had always been a tourist community, popular with fishermen and sunbathers. Dominating pier and beach, the boardwalk had been an opulent playground at the beginning of the century. John Philip Sousa played there in 1910. World War II made labor and supplies unavailable, but by 1953 Santa Cruz was on the rise again, and when Ross Gortner first saw the mile-long boardwalk, more than two and a half million dollars had been spent turning it into a neon-lit spectacular.

The walk was dominated by a monumental domed pink

building called the Coconut Grove Casino. The word DANCING flashed on and off against a pink stucco wall. Inside was a bustling penny arcade: ringing pinballs, mannequin gypsy fortune-tellers (your fortune for five cents on a calling card), bowling games and Poko-Renos. The boardwalk itself was lined with concessions: "Walking Charlie"—"Knock my hat off"; "Bazooka Guns"—destroy a tank; a rococo merry-go-round complete with calliope, and a roller coaster, roaring by every sixty-eight seconds.

By 1960 only three men were left on the boardwalk from Sousa's time. Skip Littlefield owned the Coconut Grove Casino and still worked in an oceanfront office in the building. Another old-timer made change at a booth in the penny arcade. And then there was Herbert Cunningham, concessionaire, an open, friendly man who because of his trade gave the misleading impression of being "sneaky." Cunningham's entire world was the Santa Cruz boardwalk. He loved the boardwalk life, the flow of people past the stalls, the carny catcalls of the concessionaires. He spent his life trying to get people to spend a nickel or a dime on one of his games. When Ross met him, Cunningham was a charming old huckster, always ready with a quick answer or a come-on to con the tourists out of their change. Ross took to him instantly when they met at a Nickel Pitch, and a day later Cunningham offered him a job on the boardwalk. He placed Ross behind a concession, put a microphone in his hand, and a miracle took place. The concession stand became a pulpit, and if Marjoe at six had brought the twenties rolling in for Jesus, imagine Ross's success at sixteen with dimes for a horse race.

126

The commotion in front of the Cunningham horse races drew crowds from up and down the beach. The game was simple: ten plastic horses ran across a grassy knoll, powered by ten pinball machines. The faster the balls were shot, the more quickly the horses moved. Naturally there was a gimmick: an electronic switchboard with buttons controlled by Ross. Every game had a winner, but Ross could decide who it would be.

His crafty manipulation of the buttons didn't conjure up the crowds, however. Ross's boardwalk evangelism did that.

"Right here, children of all ages, is the funniest, runniest of them all. Every game a winner. Every game a prize. Every prize a great one and you only pay a dime. Jockeys need no previous experience. Winners need no previous experience, and neither do losers. You, young lady, do *not* look like a loser. Can you beat this young man on your left?"

Ross kept the lines waiting to play. Cunningham did some quick calculating. During the day his game had been bringing in about ten dollars an hour. Ross brought in six players every minute, nonstop. That was a 350 percent increase. Like others before him, Cunningham wanted to make Ross a star, specifically a night concessionaire, for at night the crowds were larger and the prices higher. But Ross refused.

"I've got a part-time job at night."

"I'll pay you more here," Cunningham offered.

"Nope, it's family work," Ross said.

He spent cheerless nights frying hamburgers at the Pit. Marge, as charming as ever, had turned the roadside diner into a successful business. And although Ross hated being the cook, she seemed to be quieting down. For a time. Then, one Sunday night, when the diner was closed and he and Marge were cleaning up, she suggested that they give up the house in Felton.

"And move where?" Ross asked.

"In with George Curtis."

Ross liked Curtis, who had been taking a fatherly interest in him. They went fishing together on Curtis's cabin cruiser, and Curtis had even bought Ross a Colt .38 "blue lightning" pistol so that he could join a "fast-draw" club in Santa Cruz. But moving in with him . . . Too close, Ross thought.

"What about Carl Warner?"

"I can deal with him," Marge said.

Ross flared up at her. *"Mom,* you *always* . . . It just means more trouble."

She sat down across from him at the counter.

"Ross, have I ever let you down?"

"Yes," he said.

"I always tried the best I knew how," she answered stiffly. Ross softened.

"Yes, you did," he told her, and turned away. Marge addressed the wall.

"I guess you can't have everything," she sighed.

"No. Not at the same time, Mother."

But Marge tried anyway. And Ross gave her notice and took Cunningham's job as night concessionaire.

American myth is that California girls are unlike all other American women. Californians are beach people, and their children apparently emerge into the world suntanned, blond-haired, and healthy.

The California girls patroled the beach and boardwalk of Santa Cruz, flicking their long hair out of their faces and shyly eyeing the boys. At night the boardwalk became prime cruising ground, for the sexes met each other with calliope music in the background.

In the midst of all this was Ross, microphone in hand. Nobody ever asked him how old he was, assuming from his expertise and poise that he must be in his twenties. Girls on the boardwalk strolled back and forth in front of his stand, a never-ending recycling of flirtatious glances and shy smiles. For a girl to date Ross was equivalent to capturing the king of the boardwalk. Every concessionaire knew him; he and his dates could play every game for free, and ride the roller coaster on continuous shifts.

With the salary and bonuses Cunningham paid him Ross bought his own car, a Volkswagen bug. When his mother was out, he bedded his dates at home. The other nights he improved on the *Kamasutra* in the back seat of his Volkswagen and gained considerable notoriety on the boardwalk as barker and lover. His waking hours turned around, running the races till two in the morning, rising at three in the afternoon, he saw less of Marge, and then none of her at all when she finally moved into George Curtis's house.

One night at the horse races Ross gave a girl ten straight free games. She wore jeans and a work shirt and kept her hands in her pockets and tried to look tough. She pretended not to be intimidated by the famous boardwalk king. She got him to date her. Her name was Ann.

Ross didn't find her fantastically interesting, but she was pretty and he was strongly attracted to her. Their tastes were very different, except for camping in the forest. But she was the first woman besides Marge with whom he had known a real relationship and he believed, naïvely, that he was in love with her.

After Marge had met Ann she told Ross exactly what she thought of her: thick, illiterate, impolite. But he doubted if Marge would ever approve of any other woman in his life, no matter what her qualifications.

Ross and Ann almost lived in the tiny Volkswagen. They went camping in it, laughed in it, loved in it, left notes for each other in it. And one night, in the back seat, Ann informed him that she was pregnant.

"You're gonna have a baby?" Ross asked her in a tone that implied he misunderstood both her description and her condition.

Ann nodded.

"My baby?" Ross asked.

Ann, smiling, nodded again.

Ross drove her home.

During the following week Ross took her for three separate pregnancy tests to make sure it was true. For another week he tried to fathom the responsibility of fatherhood; of marriage to Ann; of life beginning for the fetus. They talked about looking for an abortionist, but that was all they did about it.

A week later, after the shock had subsided and the dread had set in, Ross told Marge.

"There must be an abortionist," said Marge.

"Maybe I should marry her," Ross suggested.

"Of course not," Marge said, getting to her feet.

"I made her pregnant."

"Well, make her *un*pregnant."

"I can't. Anyway, Ann is scared."

"Ross, *you are sixteen years old,*" Marge told him, as if he weren't painfully aware of it. "Maybe you should leave. I'll give you money to go east."

"Leave her *pregnant?* I can't."

"Why not?" Marge snapped.

"Because it's wrong. I have to marry her," Ross said.

"That's wrong," Marge shouted.

Ross put on his coat to leave the house.

Marge finally met Ann's parents. The three chatted politely and stayed together only an hour. They gave their children cash to go to Reno, Nevada. Ross drove to Reno with the determination to get it over with, as if the ceremony would end the nightmare. It only began it.

Their "honeymoon" night in Reno, in a gesture of romantic fantasy, Ross wanted to read poetry to Ann. Ann didn't like poetry. She didn't *understand* poetry, she told him. He said he would explain it, but she didn't want to listen.

Ross and Ann Gortner leased a small apartment on the outskirts of Santa Cruz. In order to pay the rent, support Ann, and save for the baby's birth, Ross again worked at Marge's Pit daylight hours and on the boardwalk at night. When he was offered a higher-paying job at the Santa Cruz Construction Company, he accepted it. The construction manager insisted that he cut his hair and although Ross didn't see any connection between laying wooden boards for poured concrete and the length of his hair, he needed the job and got a haircut.

Ann's belly blew up with a suddenness that terrified him. He prayed they wouldn't have twins.

When he read about an opening for a Standard Oil Company management trainee, he applied. He was working full time at Standard Oil when Ann went into labor. On March 2, 1961, a baby girl was born. They named her Ginny.

Home life with Ann was not painful, but it was very dull. He watched the baby asleep in the crib and tried to comprehend that the child was his. But it was just a tiny baby in a crib. He couldn't seem to make the connection.

The Standard Oil Company moved the family to Salinas, a town thirty miles inland from Santa Cruz, and then to King City, one hundred miles farther away, far away from everything. King City—population 2,000. Total isolation with Ann. Even Ross's promotion to full manager of the Standard Oil Company station didn't seem to help. He drove a hundred miles each night to take courses at the State University in Salinas, thankful for the time away from Ann and the baby.

Ross's major objection to Ann was that she didn't want to do anything. She never complained about money, or about the baby, or about Ross. She was so complacent that it doubled his unrest. He was almost eighteen, and he couldn't understand how his life had got so far off course. Each day carried him farther away from everything he dreamed of achieving. On the rare occasions when they went to visit Marge, she greeted him with a look that said "I told you so."

He fantasized constantly, not of other women or wealth or fame, but of disappearing. It was at that time, on a brief visit to Oakland, that he met Vernon's new wife, an eighteen-year-old who was a parishioner of the same church Vernon was attending. Ross was disturbed but not really surprised. He knew that as long as his father clung to his faith he would continue to deliver virtuoso performances such as this. But not long after this meeting Ross heard that the marriage had been annulled.

Shortly after his visit to Oakland, while bending down to help lift a tire in the yard at Standard Oil, Ross felt a sharp pang that started in his back and shot down his left leg. There was a blinding moment of pain, and then nothing, as if he wasn't hurt at all. Two days later he decided to see a doctor, who referred him to an orthopedic surgeon in San Francisco. It was five weeks before the diagnosis was clear. Ross had crushed the fourth lumbar disc in his back; the fragments would have to be removed and the disc wired together. In the hospital in San Francisco the doctors explained that he would probably recover completely, but he would never again be able to lift anything heavy. They added one incidental fact: he would be enclosed in a body cast, from breastbone to waist, for a minimum of six months.

Two of those months Ross spent in the hospital, and then he went home. Ann was not particularly overjoyed at the pros-

133

pect of having a semicripple around the house all day. Neither was Ross; as far as he was concerned, his family was confinement enough. The two young people already knew they had made a bad mistake, and now it seemed that they were mired in it by a twenty-pound cast as well as their marriage vows and their child. Bored with the idiocy on TV, Ross began a course of reading that was to have far-reaching consequences in his life. Ann tended to the baby or took long walks. But she never complained. If this was her life at the moment, she felt it was her duty to accept it. Ross, however, was anything but docile and the more he felt pressured by the situation, the more he fought back. The books helped.

Against doctor's orders, he drove to a nearby music store and rented an organ. When it was delivered to the house he set it up in the bedroom, not far from his bed, and for the next few months he practiced at the keyboard daily, recovering his old proficiency. He taught himself to transform gospel tunes into rock-and-roll. But after a while organ practice and his reading weren't enough to distract him from the endless waiting.

Furthermore, he was worried about money. He called his father, explaining that with the cast, the baby, and Ann, he needed some temporary financial help. But Vernon didn't seem to feel that Ross deserved any. They had had one conversation on the subject during the drive home from the San Francisco hospital. It had occurred to Ross that he had actually supported his parents for many years, and, trying not to sound like Marge, he asked Vernon where all the money went. Vernon, sounding just like Vernon, said there never was any.

Ross's relationship with Marge was no more fruitful. Things

had gone awry with George Curtis. He and Marge had disappeared to Reno for a weekend with the intention of marrying, but they returned unwed and angry. Carl Warner bought his way out of Marge's Pit. Eventually Curtis did the same. Suddenly, unannounced to Ross, Marge was married to a man she had met long ago at the Pit.

When he heard of his mother's marriage he tried to get in touch with her by phone, but the number at the diner had been disconnected. After some bedside detective work, he found a neighbor who ran into Marge almost every week and sent a message, asking her to call him. There was only cold silence. Then, after sending several letters to her old address, he finally received a phone call.

"Congratulations, Mother."

"Thank you, Ross."

"What's his name? Can I meet him?"

There was empty silence on the other end of the phone.

"Mother? Is something wrong?"

"Ross, this man I married—well, he doesn't know about me."

"Doesn't know *what?*"

"Anything. About you or the other children. I've sent Starloe to live with Vernoe and Daddy."

"You married a man who doesn't know you're an evangelist?" Ross laughed into the phone.

"The past is over with. It's dead and I'm burying it."

"And me?"

"That's buried too. For a while, anyway."

135

"Did you ever love me, Mother?"

"I sacrificed my life for you," she told him, and hung up.

When the four laborious months at home ended and the cast was removed, Ross drove to Los Angeles to look for a job. The long stretch of reading and thinking was bearing fruit. He knew they had to move from King City, and a job was a prerequisite. But the employment agencies weren't very encouraging. The areas Ross specialized in, preaching, barking, and the overall seduction of crowds, were not represented in the classifications of employment agencies, and as for gas station management, the physical labor involved made it out of the question. In any event, Ross preferred not to spend his life as a grease monkey.

On his third job-hunting trip to Los Angeles he found a classified ad for a shoe salesman.

The thought of selling shoes, kowtowing to fat old ladies, and being lost in the ranks of a large company, depressed him. But it wasn't forever, he decided, and Ann and the baby were his responsibility for the moment. He tucked his pride under his arm and filled in the job application with the best previous experience his imagination could summon up. Then he changed the date of his birth to boost his age from eighteen to twenty-three. The Innes Shoe Company hired him a week later and gave him a few weeks to relocate. Ann was overjoyed. Convinced that this was the catalyst needed to revive a dying relationship, they looked enthusiastically for a place to live. Finally they found an apartment they considered perfect: large, sunlit, and overlooking a street bustling with people. They moved almost immediately, and a week later Ross reported to work on his new job.

The Innes Shoe Stores comprised a chain of twenty-one shops in and around the Los Angeles area, and the Innes training program took itself very seriously. Ross was instructed in the manufacture of shoes, inventory, sales, and the operation of a chain. He found the program boring, full of misconceptions about people and selling techniques, but he kept his mouth shut and followed the rules of the game. He spent three months in Los Angeles as salesman, and then he was promoted to assistant manager of the Pasadena store. From Pasadena he was transferred to manage the Pico store, and not quite a year and a half later he was promoted to manager of the largest store in the chain, the Wilshire store in downtown Beverly Hills. The intelligence that had enabled the four-year-old Marjoe to field questions at a press conference was not overtaxed by the shoe business.

Time had gone by with increasing monotony. After a while every customer looked the same; so did every store. His days were mimeographed copies of one another, and the months became an arbitrary measurement that could only be counted by clearance sales or seasonal promotions. The stifling sameness of work and of home were the only realities.

The people at Innes, however, soon discovered—inevitably —that Ross had unusual sales ability. By the time he arrived at the Beverly Hills store, the home office had also found out that he was a natural at sales promotion. They liked everything about him. He began to dress in well-tailored designer suits.

137

His hair was cut by Jay Sebring. He was aloof, yet friendly. He was forceful, yet he underplayed his role. He found the salesmen and their sales policy stodgy, and he made waves trying to change them.

His first antiestablishment act was to decorate the windows with wooden orange crates. The salesmen were aghast, and warned him that the home office would have none of it. Shoes were to be displayed in sedate settings, not in crates that detracted from the shoe itself. But Ross insisted it couldn't hurt to bring a touch of pop art to the windows, and when Batman became popular as a television series, he introduced a "Bat Window." It caused a lot of attention along Wilshire Boulevard, not all of it positive, but sales increased by a third, and Ross was rewarded with a two-page story in the monthly Innes magazine. The other managers were encouraged to follow his lead.

Ann, content as always, put Ginny in nursery school and went to work at the phone company. At night she fixed dinner and they watched TV or went to an occasional movie. On Thursday nights they went shopping at the supermarket. As Ross pushed Ginny around in the grocery cart while Ann plucked cans off the shelves, he watched the other couples hypnotically following the same ritual. For a brief moment he tried to divorce himself from his physical being and stood at the other end of a long aisle, watching himself and his family leading their little lives, closed and oblivious to what was happening around them. It was a strange sensation for someone who had been a superstar at five, and who was still aware that life had more to offer.

He was nearly twenty, and they believed at work he was twenty-five. Life with Ann made him feel fifty, while right beyond his reach he saw a new society coming into being. The university campuses all around him were beginning to explode. People his age were demonstrating their sense of urgency, their determination to create a healthier world. But he was out of it. He was a married man, with a respectable job and a cute young daughter.

About this time Mexican marijuana was being smuggled into the country with improbable ease. Ross was the good friend of a twenty-seven-year-old shoe wholesaler named Vic Woodstone, and Vic had often offered to sell Ross an ounce of Acapulco gold. Ross had shrugged off the idea, but Woodstone persisted, and one night after work he turned up at the young Gortners' apartment with all the paraphernalia. Ann watched, absorbed, as Vic poured some finely shredded grass into a paper, rolled it up between his thumbs, and licked it closed. Then he lighted the joint and blew smoke at Ross. Next Ann puffed away on it while he rolled another. Soon the three of them were sitting on the floor, passing the joint back and forth.

"I don't feel a thing," Ross said. Ann laughed at him.

"What's the matter?"

"Your eyes."

"Well, I don't *feel* anything," Ross insisted. He got to his feet unsteadily and walked to the bathroom. The overhead light stung his eyes. He stood staring at himself in the mirror, examining his face. He looked tired and felt it, and without telling Vic or Ann, he made his way to the bedroom and fell

139

on the bed. Twenty minutes later Ann woke him. Vic stood in the doorway of the bedroom with his coat on.

"I've got to split," he said. "Sure you didn't feel anything?"

The salesmen at Innes, staid gentlemen in their forties, weren't very happy with the success of the new young manager. They reported to Ross with resentful hostility. They called themselves "shoe dogs," and were a basically friendly group who chaffed one another about their unenviable lot in having to deal all day with women who couldn't make up their minds. Their salaries were low, presumably because they were paid a commission on each sale. Every customer who walked through the door was jumped on by a waiting salesman, and Ross watched them play the game of getting the customer into a new pair of shoes and then out of the store as quickly as possible in order to hurry back to the door in pursuit of another commission. To move stock faster, the Innes management instituted a system of "Price Marked" or P.M. shoes. These shoes were usually poor sellers, and most of them were a few seasons old, but they earned the salesman an extra twenty-five-cent commission. The really hard-to-sell styles, some of which had been gathering dust over several seasons, were worth an extra fifty cents.

Ross knew this forced selling would lead only to chaos, and he decided to institute some new sales techniques. The other "shoe dogs" refused even to listen at first, but he laid his reputation on the line by promising them a 10 percent increase in sales if they gave the "Gortner Method" a try.

140

First, every customer was greeted with a cheerfully familiar hello.

"Good to see you," Ross would say, smiling. "How have you been?"

The customers, confused and flattered because they didn't remember the young salesman who apparently remembered them, fell into step beside him.

"Please sit down and tell me how I can help you," he would suggest. That was his second rule: every customer must be seated.

Ross knew that every woman would know her own shoe size but he insisted on measuring her foot anyway. Then, if her exact size wasn't available, he wouldn't say so but would bring out the closest size he had, which would often fit. Also, even when a woman claimed to know exactly what shoe she wanted, Ross would offer her three additional styles so that she wouldn't feel either neglected or pressured. And, when she finally made her choice, he would bring out a matching handbag and, frequently, sell it to her.

It took the older salesmen a month or two to emulate Ross's techniques; they were awkward at the beginning, and resented him even more. But gradually the "Gortner Method" began to deliver the results Ross had promised, and with increased sales, morale improved. Ross was pleased, but his satisfaction didn't affect his basic mood of dull hopelessness.

It was the year of wraparound windshields and a dance craze that swept the country with incredible speed. New York, naturally, claimed that the Peppermint Lounge was the spot in which to dance the night away. Los Angeles, naturally, adopted the idea, and eventually a club opened on the Sunset Strip called the Peppermint West.

The Peppermint West temporarily patched up the young Gortners' failing marriage. While Ross had been stimulated by the campus activists, Ann was completely indifferent to them. But they both liked to dance; they were excellent partners; and with the opening of the Peppermint West, there was finally something the two could do together. They became regulars at the club and, as new clubs opened, they followed the action up and down the Strip.

Finally the Surf Club appeared on Sunset. It turned out to be the epic club of the era. It was the best place to dance, and it provided a continuous sideshow of movie stars serving themselves from a huge buffet or squeezing past the tightly packed tables. There was a row of banquettes reserved for the famous and rich. Early-sixties psychedelia flashed on the walls, projected from hidden slide machines. And above the tiny dance floor hung two go-go cages. The owner and two maîtres d'hôtel guarded the front door, admitting and rejecting patrons as though the Surf were an exclusive private club. Ross and Ann had been going there for several weeks before they were finally recognized at the door.

When the paid go-go dancers in the cages knocked off to rest, patrons were invited to ascend into the cages and frug above the crowds. Ross and Ann were always up there and the crowd at the Surf loved them. In fact, after a few weeks of cage-dancing, the proprietor admitted them without any cover charge.

It went on like that for six months—nightly baby-sitters, rushing out to the Surf Club, dancing until the place closed, and then hurrying home for a few hours' sleep. They were six exuberant months, alive and young. For the first time in all those years, Ross was breaking loose. The six months were precious little time for him to get his fill of youth and the taste was addictive. Ann, however, began to get bored and she wanted to stay home more and more.

The first night she begged off Ross sat at home with her and sulked. By the second night she was begging him to get out of the house and leave her alone.

Solo at the Surf Club was an entirely different affair. He danced with whomever he pleased when he felt like it. When the staff man at the door took a break, Ross would cover for him, and after a few weeks he did it with some regularity. Covering the door turned out to be even more interesting than wandering around inside. He became friendly with the other regular customers, who took it for granted that he worked there. Also, he discovered that he was much more naïve than he had imagined.

The Surf Club sheltered a side business that Ross had never suspected. He discovered its existence simply enough one night when a man stuck a twenty-dollar bill in his hand and asked him to set up a date with a particular waitress.

"Ask her yourself," Ross told him, shoving the bill back. The man whispered in Ross's ear.

"Ask her for me; I'm kind of shy."

So Ross called the waitress aside and told her the man wanted a date. She thanked him and the matter was apparently forgotten. But two nights later, when Ross was at the door again, the waitress breezed by and said, "Thanks; I made fifty bucks."

After that Ross refused to perform the same service when patrons of the club approached him. But he found out soon enough that the waitresses were angry with him. He finally mentioned the problem to the proprietor.

"Look, kid, what goes on outside of this place is not my business. It's not your business. We're here to make people feel comfortable. We take tips to give a guest a ringside table, right? If a guy's bashful and all you have to do is point him out to the girl, what's so wrong with that? Make yourself an extra couple of bucks."

So Ross became a part-time pimp.

Five years of his life seemed to have disappeared into a void. Only later would he realize how valuable those years had been. His world was bounded by a shoe store and a bad marriage, and he clung to the Surf Club as to a life preserver. Hundreds of miles away, the woman who once ruled his life was silent. Her marriage was apparently successful, and she continued to ignore her family. Ross thought of her often, and he wondered what Marge would think if she could see him as he had become. He lived in a house in the Valley. There was a color TV, a black Cadillac, and a barbecue in the back yard. Yet the ego and the passion of his childhood had seemed to promise something else. Contentment, ardor, hope . . . he felt none of them. Frustrated and dissatisfied, he grew further away from Ann. Discontent changed to dislike. Ginny suffered the most, and Ross was painfully aware of it. He and Ann discussed divorce daily, but she didn't understand why things couldn't be worked out. And Ross couldn't communicate with her well enough to explain.

CHAPTER 7

The Surf Club had communicants as devoted to it as Marjoe's congregations had been to religion. They were all types: pompous show-offs, starlets, those who came to ogle the movie stars, and the idle rich. Executives of the major studios brought their wives; people came to see and be seen. Ross observed them with indifference.

It was not unusual to see an older man accompanying a younger, attractive woman, but there was one particular couple, a man in his late sixties and a wife in her early forties, whom Ross did mull over. They came to the Surf twice a week, arriving in a white Rolls-Royce, and the chauffeur would wait outside for them until they were ready to leave. Their reservations were made under the name of Georgeson. Mrs. Georgeson, Ross thought, was a marvelous-looking woman. He guessed her age at forty-two, but she looked more like thirty-five. When she smiled, as she always did when Ross greeted them, her face radiated contentment and warmth. Mr. Georgeson, distinguished, silver-haired, conservatively dressed, would nod abruptly. Ross supposed that escorting Mrs.

146

Georgeson to the Surf Club was a burdensome chore for her husband. He quite obviously felt, and looked, out of place.

Ross had seen them at the club at least twenty times before he had his first, and only, conversation with Mr. Georgeson. He was standing in the men's room, when Mr. Georgeson entered. He looked glum and kept his hands in his pockets.

"You know my wife, son?"

"Yes, Mr. Georgeson."

Georgeson removed his right hand from his pocket and stuck something in the breast pocket of Ross's jacket.

"Please . . ." He paused, fumbling for words. "Would you dance with her, please?"

Ross didn't think he'd heard correctly. He began to ask him to repeat the sentence.

"I'm sorry, but I don't—"

"Please," Georgeson interrupted. "Don't say no. I'm too tired for all this dancing." He turned quickly and left the men's room. Ross started after him but stopped to check his breast pocket. It held a fifty-dollar bill.

He pushed past the crowds of people on the dance floor and saw Mrs. Georgeson sitting alone at her table. Hesitantly he went over to her and stood there, peering down at her.

"Would you care to dance?"

Ross was fascinated by Mrs. Georgeson on the dance floor. He compared her with Ann, and decided Mrs. Georgeson was the better dancer. She kept smiling; they continued to dance; and after about half an hour she suggested they leave.

"I promised I'd hang around for another half hour. Then,

147

if you want to, I'll drive you home. I have to tell you something," Ross said.

"All right. I'll wait," she answered, as if it was nothing unusual.

Ross spent a half hour at the door, then got his black Cadillac and pulled it up front. Mrs. Georgeson was waiting. One of the carhops opened the door for her and she got in. Traffic was light and they moved quickly up the Strip.

"Where do you live?" Ross asked.

"The Beverly Hills Hotel," she said.

"You *live* at the Beverly Hills Hotel?"

He heard a cheerful sweet sound and realized she was laughing. He kept glancing anxiously at her.

"I have something to tell you," he finally said.

"What?" She stuck her chin out and her nose up, indicating he could say anything and it wouldn't faze her in the least.

"Mr. Georgeson gave me fifty dollars to dance with you."

"Oh, I know," she said.

"You *know* I got paid to dance with you and you don't care? Doesn't it make you feel a little *cheap?* What does he think of you anyhow?"

"I'm not sure what he thinks. But I'll explain it all at the hotel."

They pulled up in the driveway of the hotel. Two attendants ran to the car doors.

"Ross, I don't *live* here."

"Well, then, what the hell—"

"Give me back the fifty," she said.

He handed it to her.

148

"Feel better?" she asked.

Ross nodded.

"All right, then. At least have a drink with me."

She got out of the car and walked into the hotel. Ross hesitated for a moment, but followed her.

They sat in a corner of the Polo Lounge, ordered drinks, chatted about the Surf Club for a while. Then Mrs. Georgeson lowered her voice.

"I think I owe you an explanation, only I think it's too soon."

"I don't," Ross declared, beginning to feel a tiny bit drunk.

"All right," Mrs. Georgeson said. "First of all, please call me Joanne. Mrs. Georgeson makes me feel ancient."

Ross conceded. "Joanne," he said.

She lighted a cigarette.

"That was *my* fifty Gregory gave you." Ross looked baffled for a second.

"Gregory is Mr. Georgeson," she explained.

"Look, I don't know what your arrangement with your husband is. I don't care. But I'm no hustler."

"I didn't think you could be bought. You don't even look the type." She laughed, and for some reason he couldn't understand, he laughed with her.

"I *figured* that fifty would insult you. Look, it was a cheap trick, I admit, but it *did* get your attention."

"What about Mr. Georgeson? How does he feel about it?"

It was obviously a good question. Joanne took a sip of her drink and thought it over.

"Ross, Gregory and I—well, we love each other—in our own way. I don't know how that fifty made him feel. He's been

149

married three times before. He got *taken* three times before. Large alimony and all that. There are things about our life that are perfect—I make a good home for him, I entertain well, I'm respectable. I have my own career and a good job at the studio. Gregory and I are good friends. We're marvelous friends, and that's the most important thing in a marriage."

Ross flashed on Ann and his little girl.

"Listen, do you play tennis?"

"Yes, I love to," Ross answered.

"Well, Gregory doesn't play tennis and doesn't *want* to play tennis. Gregory doesn't dance. I love to dance." She paused, smiling.

Ross looked down at his drink. "Why me?" he asked.

Then she laughed again. She moved her hand to his arm, touching him very lightly.

Several hours later they were dressing in a room at the hotel. It was five in the morning.

"I want to be home to have breakfast with Gregory," Joanne said. "Will you drop me off? It's only down Beverly Glen Drive. But I can take a taxi. . . ."

"No. Sure, I can drop you off."

"Where do you live? Where do you go from here?"

"Home. The Valley," Ross said. As an afterthought he added, "Wife and kid."

Joanne stopped dressing.

"You're married! Why didn't you tell me?"

"Why should I?"

They were silent until Ross drove her up a circular driveway to a pseudo-Tudor mansion. Joanne turned and touched his arm again.

"Sunday, at ten. I'll meet you at the courts."

She gave him the address, and then briskly left the car and entered the house.

Ross couldn't look at Ann when he got home. She was asleep in a disheveled bed. He peeked in Ginny's room and then walked to the small bed she slept in. Maybe one day we can be friends too, he thought.

"Over my dead body," Ann told him the next day when he came home from Innes. "Sunday is the only day I get to do anything. You and your friends can run around on your own time—I want you home on Sunday."

"Let's stop," Joanne shouted to him from across the net. Ross walked to the side of the court. Joanne took his arm as they headed for the bench.

"Why don't we get out of these clothes and have lunch?"

They met by his car twenty minutes later.

"Big black Cadillac!" she teased him. "Where do you want to have lunch? It's on me."

"On you? I pay when I go out."

"I realize this is a Cadillac, but I don't think you can afford my tastes. Is this car paid for?"

"Of course," he said, pulling onto the freeway.

"Do they pay that much at the Surf Club?"

"The club's only a diversion for me. I have a full-time job during the day."

When he told her he was manager of the Wilshire Innes, she gulped.

"Then I must have seen you there a dozen times!" She paused. "And the Surf is to get away from your wife?"

Ross nodded.

"Well, I'm glad to hear you're doing so well, but lunch is still on me."

During lunch Joanne told him about her own career. Years before, she had been a seamstress and then a wardrobe mistress. Eventually she had started designing costumes, and thanks to a little bit of studio politics she had got a chance to do the costumes for a splashy contemporary film with a big budget. Gregory was her first husband. She had never seen any reason for marriage before, but Gregory needed to be sure of her, and she herself discovered, to her surprise, that she wanted a certain kind of stability. They had been married eight years.

Three weeks later Ann exploded.

"You're cheating on me," she cried.

"Ann, we've got nothing to cheat on."

"I won't give you a divorce."

"It doesn't matter. I don't want to get married. Listen, I know I'm not here a lot. I won't go to the Surf Club if it'll make you feel better."

It seemed to satisfy her for a while.

Joanne rented a nondescript apartment on La Cienega Boulevard, but they never stayed there overnight. She always returned to Gregory before he woke in the morning. And Ross went home to Ann. Only once did they get to spend three uninterrupted days together, when Joanne flew them down to Acapulco so that they could visit the set of a movie she had worked on.

The time he spent with her softened his judgment of many people, including his parents. He laughed more. Marge had brainwashed him to believe that people were always out to get one another; Joanne taught him that some could be trusted and some could not.

Ann, conversely, became more alienated. She never really knew about his affair with Joanne, whatever she may have suspected, but she could not fail to realize his emotional withdrawal. Ross's chief fear was that Ginny would be harmed by the disintegrating relationship.

He tried not to discuss his marital problems with Joanne, just as she rarely mentioned Gregory to him. But after they had known each other nearly a year, he told her something of his anxieties.

"You know what you need?" Joanne asked as he drove her home one night.

"I need a divorce," he said.

Joanne ignored him. "You need a hobby."

"A hobby. Oh, great."

"There must be something you've wanted to do and haven't done. I don't know what men like to do in their spare time. Build something. Build a doghouse."

"I haven't got a dog," Ross said. "Why don't *you* have a hobby?"

"Oh, I do." She smiled her overpowering warm smile. "You're my hobby," she said, and hopped out of the car.

Ross had never been offended by anything Joanne said, but her "hobby" remark echoed disturbingly through his mind the next day. It may have had something to do with the decision he made soon after.

The first step was to buy an organ and begin practicing again. The next step was Wallach's Music City, the supermarket of the tune industry in Los Angeles. For an unemployed musician without union membership, it was the equivalent of Schwab's drugstore. There was a large bulletin board where instrumentalists advertised their availability and that also carried listings of bands that needed one or two musicians to fill out the ensemble.

It would have been easiest for Ross to join a pre-existing group that was looking for an organist, but he stuck to being a self-starter, and what he really wanted was to create his own band. He took from the board the name of every available musician.

He didn't mention the idea to Ann, but she heard him making phone calls in the kitchen, and she sauntered up to stand in the doorway, arms crossed on her chest.

"What's up?"

"What's what?" Ross said, dialing again.

"All the phone calls?"

"I'm starting a band."

154

"Oh," she said, and disappeared into the bedroom. Somehow her lack of interest infuriated him. But at least he finally felt angry rather than discouraged, and that made him somewhat optimistic.

Musicians started arriving at the house a week later, auditioning, talking, jamming together. At first Ann paid no attention, but after a few nights she began to enjoy having the strangers around, and she became friendlier and even flirtatious.

The musicians themselves were only fair to middling. Most good musicians either were already in bands or belonged to the local union, and the men Ross finally selected for his group were strictly nonprofessional. Nonmusical, too, but he intended to change that although he knew it would be no small feat. Through it all he kept reminding himself that it was all supposed to be only a hobby.

Lead guitarist of the group was Steve Klein, a confident youth of twenty-three with bushy hair growing around his ears and down the back of his neck. Steve Klein had a wife and child and no job, yet he never seemed to need any money. He also had a series of unexplained appointments which interrupted rehearsals. Steve obviously had no special musical ability, but Ross enjoyed his mysteriousness enough to keep him in the group.

They changed drummers three times before Klein introduced a boy named Sparky Jaffe. Sparky touted himself as a great drummer but he always had an excuse for not being up to par. He was either hung over, or suffering from some arthritic condition. Ross would have to show him how to do the drum riffs. Sparky would say, "Sure, I know it. Just not today. I'll do it tomorrow."

Ross's third acquisition was a sleepy-looking boy named Andrew Leigh, who played bass guitar, or at least claimed to play bass guitar. Originally Andrew boasted of his proficiency on every instrument, but Ross finally had him audition for bass guitar. He wasn't bad, but he never again played as well as at the audition. Instead he tried to convince everyone else to let him play *their* instruments.

After one month of rehearsal with this hopeless assortment, Ross begged a date at a small club downtown. The night before, they sat around the living room of Ross's house trying to figure out a name for the group. Ann passed through the room, heading toward the kitchen, when Ross came up with the name "Grim Reapers."

The harvest of their first date was naught. After their first song the manager asked them to stop playing and leave the club. Ross told the story to Joanne the next night as she was about to leave their apartment on La Cienega. She laughed and told him to practice fortitude.

"The past year and a half would have been lousy without you," Ross told her. She didn't answer him. He got up from the bed, helped zip up the back of her dress, and kissed her. But she didn't kiss him back. Instead she began to speak in a businesslike tone.

"You know . . . let's not get too dependent on each other. Now don't be hurt," she quickly added.

"Joanne, I'm an extremely independent person. I always have been."

156

"I guess you probably are," she sighed, "but maybe I'm not."

He saw Joanne only twice after that. The last time, they had dinner in a tiny restaurant she especially liked. She talked about the band and the shoe store, systematically refusing to be drawn into a discussion of their previous conversation. Later that night he felt like a stranger with her.

Although he couldn't then admit it to himself, the abrupt end of his relationship with Joanne led directly to the abrupt end of his marriage. Joanne had leveled out his life. Elusive though their affair had been, it was the only healthy relationship he had known. With Joanne gone, life with Ann was like a desert, a dry and barren expanse dotted with prickly growth. They hadn't made love in months. All communication between them had stopped. And suddenly Ann, indolent, indifferent Ann, reached the point where she too knew it was time to separate and begin her own life.

He offered to find an apartment for himself but Ann refused to remain alone in the large house, and so the following Sunday he drove around Los Angeles and turned up three apartments for her to choose from. He settled back to wait while she made up her mind, assuming it would take weeks, but she picked the one she wanted immediately and moved out the next day.

Ross didn't mind living alone, but the house seemed cold and empty.

Spring arrived, and this time the city actually seemed to change and flower around him. The hippies began to arrive and the new counterculture surrounded him in the streets, on TV, and in the papers. Although he had been smoking grass for several years, he wasn't a habitual user, or "head," and acid was not especially popular among his friends. Or so he thought before Steve Klein moved in with him. The mysterious Klein had broken up with his wife, loaded his belongings into his old car, and dropped by the house one night to ask Ross if he could stay until he found his own place.

Klein had been there only two days when he produced a tab of acid as a gift for Ross. Ross had been reading about Timothy Leary and was curious. He dropped the tab. He dropped acid that day and several other times during the next two months. He played with the band while he was tripping and went to work tripping. He saw people stripped of their defenses, forced within themselves. He understood for the first time what the word Karma meant. His reading began to fit into place.

Klein kept a steady stream of clients coming in and out of the house.

Ross began to find things missing. Clothes disappeared, the refrigerator was always empty, and people were always asleep in his bed. Before he knew it, the house had turned into a communal crash pad. The typical crasher was so long-haired Ross looked conservative by comparison, and it was possible to stay stoned all day for free just by sitting in the house.

Ross finally told Klein that he didn't want all the drug freaks in and out of his house. Klein would have to find another place for his menagerie. As an afterthought, he told him he could stay in the garage until he found a place of his own. But as soon as Klein moved into the garage, people started breaking into the house, eating all the food or throwing it around, ringing the bell all night, looking for drugs. At the store, the salesmen observed that Ross often looked tired and even slightly bedraggled. He became a private person. He never saw the people he had known with Ann. He bought a Great Dane puppy to keep him company. But he wasn't content. The Grim Reapers were his only relaxation. He met women at the clubs and found them boring. He never spoke to his family. He began to feel as though he was shrinking inwardly instead of expanding. He stopped taking acid. He traded the Cadillac for a Volkswagen bus. He took Briar, the Great Dane, for long walks. His life lay behind him. There was no future now. Just one day following the next. He understood what Marge had felt at the Felton diner.

CHAPTER 8

They called it the "San Francisco summer" and made famous the intersection of Haight and Ashbury streets. From across the nation an army of young nomads drifted west.

While the element could be localized in San Francisco, all of Los Angeles was invaded. The streets were lined with homeless and hungry teen-agers, selling copies of the *Free Press* for a dime. "Turning on" was suddenly a way of life, and restaurants put signs in their windows: NO BARE FEET ALLOWED. It was in the early spring of 1967 that Stephanie Hollander was drawn to Los Angeles by the fantasy of freedom. She had been born twenty-four years before in Beaufort, South Carolina, the only child of middle-aged parents. Wide-eyed, blue-eyed, an Alice perpetually in search of Wonderland, she hated the blank horizons of her home place.

Her mother and father, adoring their change-of-life child, bred her as a fine French goose is bred for pâté and ordained her destiny as teacher and wife. But at nineteen, after only one year of college, she abruptly decided to follow her White Rabbit and move to New York.

The Hollanders were horrified at the thought of Stephanie in the city, alone and unprotected, but she gave them little opportunity to object. With characteristic suddenness she was gone, and her parents heard nothing from her until she had settled in a small apartment on New York's upper East Side. Trying to nestle into the New York she imagined, she lost track of her parents, her past, and her dreams.

It wasn't until four years later, when flower power was being propagandized all around her, that she realized she had become a member of the establishment and thus an enemy of the "people." The establishment, to be sure, was not the narrow-minded Beaufort she had run away from, but it was no rabbit hole either. Her New York existence was a structured maze, dictating its own rigid standards.

With this in mind, she bought herself a pair of granny glasses to replace her horn-rimmed ones, and with her mongrel puppy Thruppence at her heels, she arrived in Los Angeles to become one of the beautiful people.

Stephanie bought a copy of the *Los Angeles Times* at the airport and asked the taxi driver to take her directly to a furnished apartment listed in the classifieds. The cab stopped on a block lined with pink, blue, and white buildings, all with carports tucked under the second floor. She climbed a steep flight of metal steps to ring the landlord's bell and asked to see the available apartment. An hour later she was alone in apartment 5, third floor rear. Thruppence clawed at the electric blue wall-to-wall carpeting. The furniture was functional, antiseptic, and antisocial. For the first time she felt very much alone.

Counting out the cash in her purse, she allocated seventy-five dollars to new clothes and some personal touches for the apartment. She put the remaining sixty dollars in a plastic canister marked "Flour" and left the apartment to find adventure in the streets of Los Angeles. All she found was Fairfax Avenue, broad and streaming with ethnic vitality. She stopped at a narrow store, The Psychedelia, parceled between a fruit stand and a John's Bargain Store. Inside, she purchased a box of incense and a poster of Timothy Leary. Then she took a bus up Fairfax until it passed Wilshire Boulevard. She wandered back to the shopping district and bought a pair of jeans and a tie-dyed T-shirt. Satisfied that she had taken the initial steps to becoming a flower child, she returned to the apartment and waited, but nothing happened.

She spent the next two weeks hitchhiking to the beach, and acquired a dark tan and sun-bleached hair. In appearance she fit the California stereotype perfectly, yet in the two weeks she lay on the beach she never met anyone, and each evening she returned to her apartment to read the papers and watch television.

In thinking out a solution to her problem, Stephanie decided her life most lacked a specific casualness of attitude. Resolved to change, she left the doors unlocked and smiled at strangers in the street. One morning she stepped out of the shower, wrapped herself in a white terry-cloth robe, and found a young man sitting in her kitchen drinking instant coffee. Back in New York, Stephanie thought, this would have been nervous-breakdown time.

"What are you doing here?" she asked.

"The door was open and when I saw you get up I thought I'd come over and join you for coffee," she was told from behind a shaggy beard. Stephanie lit a cigarette and tried to be nonchalant. She poured boiling water in her cup and nodded at the silent stranger, who sipped his coffee and smiled.

"How did you see me get up?" she asked finally.

"From there." He pointed to the apartment building next door. "From my bedroom windows."

Stephanie peered through the kitchen curtains at the pink building fifteen feet away and made a mental note that casualness need not include exhibitionism. Hereafter her bedroom blinds would be tightly drawn.

"Well," she said, sitting across from him. "my name is Stephanie Hollander."

"Mine's John. What's your sign?"

"I don't know. April twenty-third, whatever that is."

"Taurus," John said, brightening. "You must be a pretty sensual person."

"Oh, yeah." Stephanie shrugged, and then she slurped her instant coffee, feeling all interest in the hippie culture ebbing.

"Let's truck on down to my uncle's place and eat lunch for free," John suggested.

He brought her to a little restaurant in downtown Beverly Hills. As soon as they sat down, John's uncle started complaining about the lack of help. Stephanie suddenly spouted, "I need a job."

"Experience," the uncle told her solemnly from across the table. "What I need is experience."

"I have experience," Stephanie lied. "In New York I worked as a waitress." The uncle looked dubious for a moment. "All right. We'll see. Tomorrow, come in at eleven."

Late that evening, after thanking John and sending him home with a handshake, she practiced carrying dishes around her kitchen and decided she had made a great deal of progress in one day.

She carried trays and dishes filled with eggs and ham. She spilled orange juice and watched the bacon slide off the plates onto the laps of customers. She ordered sandwiches with mayonnaise instead of mustard. The smell of dirty dishes in the kitchen made her sick.

By two o'clock in the afternoon John's uncle was beckoning Stephanie aside.

"This is the first time you've done this kind of work, no?"

"No, it isn't. In New York . . ." she began, but she was too tired to lie and just shrugged her shoulders.

The uncle softened a bit. "Experience. All I ever ask for is experience. If a girl really wants work, I'll give her work. You're demoted to cashier."

Stephanie arrived on time for the next three weeks and spent her days inserting checks into a slot and punching keys. Twice she tallied up three dollars short, which she made up from her own money. Five times she tallied over the daily amount. Eventually the uncle was beckoning her aside again.

"Stephanie, Stephanie," he said, wiping his palms on his pants. "Stephanie, you're a sweet girl but you're fired."

She sighed, but it was a sigh of relief. "Don't worry," the

uncle assured her. "You'll find a nice young man and get married."

When the day was over she was apologetically handed a pay check that included a small bonus. Feigning total bliss, she thanked the uncle and shuffled out into the hot streets. At a bus stop she sat on a bench which was a billboard for the Forest Lawn Cemetery and stared dumbly at the smog.

It was too late to hitch to the beach and too early to feed Thruppence. "Well, spend some money!" she told herself, and swiveled around on the bench to look for a store. The Innes Shoe Store was right behind her. "Shoes are as good as anything," she decided, and walked up to the window. She spotted a pair of white patent shoes on the left side. With her pay check in her pocket, and her depression swiftly receding, she passed through the double doors into the air-conditioned store and rammed right into a man.

"Oh, I'm sorry!" She giggled nervously. Stephanie looked up at Ross Gortner, almost a foot taller than she. He smiled at her, blue eyes crinkling at the corners.

"My dear, that was the nicest accident I've had all day. Excuse me." Stephanie nodded and wandered off through the store. I let all the good ones get away, she decided. A thin salesman in his late forties approached her.

"Madam, may *I* be of service?"

Stephanie told him her shoe size and sat down, having pointed out the patent shoes in the window. "But only a moment, madam," the salesman said, and vanished. In ten minutes he returned with five pairs of shoes. When Stephanie finally convinced him that she wanted only the patent leather pair and did not want a matching pocketbook, he took her shoes to the cash register to make out the sales slip. Stephanie followed him and produced the pay check.

"Oh, my dear lady—why didn't you tell me this before?" he moaned, waving the check at her.

"I didn't know you needed to know before," she told him innocently. He sighed. "No third-party checks, madam," and started off with the shoes.

"Hey, wait a minute!" Stephanie shouted after him, her acquired New York aggression sprouting from behind her California insouciance. "Don't just walk away like that! I want to see the manager."

The salesman was flabbergasted. "Madam, I can assure you I'm fully aware of the store policy."

"Can I help, Mr. Denke?" someone asked.

"Oh, Mr. Ross! Tell this lady the store policy about third-party checks."

Mr. Denke triumphantly folded his arms across his chest and glared at her. Mr. Ross took her by the arm, moved her away from Mr. Denke, and sat her down in a chair. Suddenly she found herself telling him the entire story of the restaurant, the uncle, being fired, and wanting the shoes to cheer herself up. Ross Gortner sat patiently in the seat next to her until the end of the story, smiling as she went on, not missing an inch of her. Then he said, "All right. I think I'll take a chance on you." Stephanie caught the double meaning but decided to ignore it. She thought he was charming, but his well-tailored suit and suave manner didn't exactly fit her image of a hippie guru. And a shoe store manager, she thought. "What a boring life he leads!"

Ross noted her home address and phone number on the back of the check. He cashed it and handed her the shoes and the change. She filled her empty purse and shook hands formally. Leaving him behind at the double doors, she raced to the corner and boarded the approaching Fairfax Avenue bus.

Her next stop was The Psychedelia. Stephanie had been making weekly purchases of incense there, and discussing the "revolution" with the pimply-faced boy behind the counter. She was in the rear of the store when the door opened and Ross Gortner walked inside, giving the boy behind the counter a big hello. Stephanie decided not to notice him, but he lingered by the counter so long that she finally had to confront him.

"Hello again!" he said.

Stephanie nodded and paid for her purchases.

"What a coincidence!" Ross remarked.

"Yes, small world," Stephanie said to him. He raised his eyebrows and smiled. Stephanie took her package and brushed past him without speaking. He sure does get around, she thought, and began to walk home briskly, trying to figure out why she was giving him such a hard time. "You can't tell a book by its cover," she kept telling herself.

She heard Thruppence clawing at the apartment door as she came up the stairs. She sat on the carpeting next to him and scratched behind his ears. "You're shaggy enough for me," she told him. "Let's go for a walk." The brown furry dog rushed down the steps, his leash trailing behind him. Stephanie fumbled with her keys at the door, shouting, "Thruppence, come here!" but he was halfway down the block by the time she reached the street. In the distance she could see him prancing around a kneeling figure. Stephanie broke into a trot, calling "Thruppence, Thruppence!" until she was close enough to recognize Ross Gortner playing with her dog.

"You're following me, aren't you?" she said to him.

"Yes. Aren't you complimented? I left work and came all the way over here just to play with your dog."

Stephanie laughed. "Thruppence appreciates it. Aren't they going to miss you at the store?"

"Not for a while, anyway. Let's talk for a minute."

He led her to the fender of a parked car. They sat there and talked for almost an hour. She told him how she had come to Los Angeles from New York, and admonished herself for being so chatty with him for the second time that day. And she admitted she found life in Los Angeles dull, except for the moment she found John sitting in her kitchen.

"Do you like surprises?" he asked.

"More surprises? What's this one?"

"It happens night after next, at eight o'clock. Are you up for it?"

"I *really* don't usually go out with strangers. In New York—" she began to lecture.

"This is Los Angeles," Ross interrupted, "where you have coffee with potential rapists and terrific dates with shoe store managers. Agreed?"

Stephanie nodded. Ross put his fingertips on her forehead.

"Bless you, my child," he said, and sauntered off down the street.

When Ross arrived at her apartment two nights later, Stephanie found it hard to believe it was the same man. His hair, which had been brushed back two days before, was now shaggy and fell in curls around his ears. He wore a pair of old jeans, boots, and a work shirt.

"You look fabulous!" she told him.

"I'm supposed to tell *you* that."

"It's just that at the shoe store—"

"That's work," Ross said. "Tonight is play."

She locked Thruppence in the apartment and followed him downstairs to a double-parked Volkswagen bus. As they drove to the Santa Monica beach, Ross revealed his "surprise."

"We're called the Grim Reapers. I got the band together about a year ago."

"Are you good?" Stephanie asked.

"Actually, we're pretty grim. I'm organist and singer."

"Great. I can't wait. I've never been out with a musician before."

"Wait until you hear us before you decide we're musicians."

"Are you from California?" she asked.

"Yes. Long Beach."

"I'd love to go out there, to the boardwalk. Are your parents living there?"

"No," he said. Then there was a long silence. Stephanie decided she wouldn't ask any more questions.

169

There was a large marquee in front of a wooden building on the edge of the beach. The marquee was lighted with bright red letters: TONIGHT—THE GRIM REAPERS. Two members of the band were standing in the parking lot with their girls. Ross quickly introduced Stephanie and then went inside the club to set up.

Stephanie looked around the large room and everyone looked the same: tanned blond surfers and tanned blond girls. Their heads bobbed up and down on the dance floor, a pulsating wave. Abruptly, the record they were dancing to ended. Up on the stage Ross sat behind a miniature electric organ. The houselights dimmed and the stage was bathed in a deep pink glow. Stephanie felt a chill of anticipation and pride as an invisible announcer said, "And now, the incredible sounds of the Grim Reapers!" The group bolted into their first number, and Stephanie realized they were truly incredible.

They were awful. Instead of playing together they played against each other. The bass guitar lagged behind the rest, the drummer couldn't find a rhythm to stay with. One of the girls across the table from her gave Stephanie a knowing look, then held a finger up in the air, suggesting that she wait a minute. The crowd out front was noisy and hostile. Nobody danced. Then Ross jumped up from the keyboard and grabbed a microphone. He seemed to hold it perfectly, a relaxed extension of his body, as if he had always held a microphone. His voice, now singing solo, was firmly pitched yet finely grained. He gained momentum with each lyric, his strength pulling the guitarist into beat, giving the drummer a broad beam of rhythm to hang

170

from. The club grew still and attentive. Ross continued song after song as the dance floor filled with people, building to a frenzied pitch. Finally the set ended. Stephanie stood to see Ross, through the smoke and colored lights, drenched in sweat and grinning broadly at the audience.

As a recording came back on over the amplifiers, she pushed her way across the crowded room to find him.

He took her hand and slipped out a side door. They stood on a wide wooden deck overlooking the Pacific. A few couples leaned along the railing, necking or watching the moon shimmer on the waves.

"That was great," Stephanie finally brought herself to say. She realized she was trembling, that she was strangely in awe of him.

He stared out to the ocean, and Stephanie remained silent. She hoped for a while that he would put his arms around her, that she could kiss him and begin to show him what she felt, but she saw that he was far away, so far that the expanse of the Pacific seemed small for a moment.

Stephanie found Ross different from all the other men she had known. First of all he didn't grapple her home to bed that first night or on their two dates that followed. He was courteous and attentive, without any trace of the macho bravado that bored her in most men. But he was exciting to be with and she loved his romanticism and his unabashed tenderness.

On their second date he stowed two bicycles inside the Volkswagen bus and drove along the ridge of the mountains that made up the city's backbone and through the Malibu

171

canyon. He parked the bus by the side of the road and they bicycled up Route 1 in the balmy ocean air. When they stopped at a deserted beach, he unstrapped his bicycle basket and they walked along the sand. Dinner and a bottle of wine emerged from the basket and after dinner they sat on the beach, Stephanie digging up mounds of sand in her hands and watching tiny sand crabs scurry back into the white grains.

At the end of their fourth date, she sat in the passenger seat of the bus and watched the beam of the headlights cut through pellets of rain. Neither of them had spoken for several minutes, and a sudden surge of anxiety ran through her.

Am I ever going to sleep with him? she wondered. Maybe he doesn't like me. Maybe he's not even attracted to me. Maybe . . .

"Would you like to have some tea at my house?" he asked. Stephanie nodded.

"Why don't you bring your dog? He can play with my Great Dane."

"Will we be long?" she asked, prodding, pushing. He smiled.

Auspiciously enough, Stephanie woke the next morning to find Thruppence and the Great Dane, Briar, sitting on a mound of shredded foam that had once been the living room sofa.

Life in Los Angeles now became everything Stephanie had hoped for. She and Ross often traveled up the coast in his bus and slept in a tent under the redwoods, and when the Monterey Pop Festival was announced, they made plans to spend the weekend at a campsite nearby. The night they left for Monterey, they stopped outside the Esalen Institute.

"Want to take a hot bath?"

They carried towels with them to a high fence by the edge of the road. Ross helped Stephanie climb over. They undressed and ran down a steep incline wrapped in their towels. They spent an hour giggling in the smoky baths, and when they emerged they heard strange, twangy music nearby. Dressing hurriedly, they followed the sounds to an open field where forty or fifty people sat clustered around an Indian in white flowing robes.

It was Ravi Shankar.

Ross and Stephanie sank to the ground and listened. The couple next to them passed a joint and they lay back, surrounded by the sounds of the sitar, watching the stars gleam against the blue-ink sky.

The next day Ravi Shankar played at the Monterey Pop Festival, along with Janis Joplin and Jimi Hendrix. Stephanie and Ross wandered through the throngs of people. For two days they lived on hot dogs and orange drinks and excitement.

Ross opened a small plastic cube sitting on the coffee table.

"I have here two of the very best tabs of Owsley acid that exist in all of Southern California. And the price of admission is only your mind."

Stephanie took a tab from the palm of his hand and popped it in her mouth.

After a while Ross suggested they go outside. "I want to take you somewhere really special."

The headlights and the freeways oozed by them like runny eggs as Ross drove to the Transcendental Meditation Center in Malibu. The gates were locked.

"Up over the fence?" Stephanie suggested.

Ross helped her inside, then scurried over. The Center was a maze of gardens and streams, crisscrossed with tiny bridges. On one side were the mountains, to the west the Pacific. They lay under a tree until dawn.

"You know what?" Stephanie told him. "You glow."

"I glow? It's an hallucination," Ross assured her.

"I know it's an hallucination, but nobody else we saw glows. You glow silver. It's all around your body like a halo." And when she looked at his face she saw the impish face of a child, a small boy locked inside a man.

As the sun came up, she stared into his eyes to see the dawn reflected in the irises.

They decided to rent another house. It was already early fall as they read the classifieds daily for an available place. The fourth house they looked at was a small cottage on a hill above a large, incredible mansion—a mansion so incredible Stephanie thought Ross wanted the smaller one in order to see the larger. The amazing house, enormous as it was, had been built completely by hand. Its owner, Maxwell Van Rellin, had been a master shipbuilder during World War I and had settled in Hollywood during the 1920s after marrying a silent-film star. While they lived in another house in Beverly Hills, Van Rellin spent his days building his dream house himself. It looked more like a ship than a house. Each beam and slat was hand cut and fitted. No nails had been used and the whole building was hand pegged.

When Ross and Stephanie first rang Van Rellin's doorbell, a prim elderly woman invited them in. She greeted the young couple formally but with warmth. Ross introduced himself and explained that he wanted to see the small house. The woman asked them to wait in a large sitting room while she told Van Rellin they were there. Then, in introducing them to Van Rellin, she called them "Mr. and Mrs. Gortner." Stephanie smiled at the mistake, but Ross considered it a fortunate one. Van Rellin was reluctant about renting the smaller house, and Ross was almost certain he would have refused if he had thought they weren't married.

Ross had a wonderful rapport with Van Rellin from the second they met. He asked question after question about the ship-house, and all three toured it together. The upper stories were dotted with ship portals; all the wood inside was highly polished; every door and closet was fitted with brass marine hardware. Stephanie was exhausted when they were finally shown the house they had come to see, but she was certain by then that Ross would want to live there. It was a Spanish cottage that had once been the guest house. Nearby was an old aviary filled with large plants and trees.

By the time they got around to talking about money, Van Rellin was so impressed with Ross that he knocked fifty dollars off the rent. They parted late that night, and moved into the house on the first of the month.

175

Almost every night after dinner, Ross walked down the road and talked with Van Rellin for an hour or so. It turned out that Van Rellin's father had been a minister, and Ross found Van Rellin the perfect sounding board for his slowly clarifying ideas about God. The contradictions in Ross's own life had started him on a search for an acceptable answer; the intensity of that search was responsible for his voracious reading; but essentially what he learned from his books was that almost every religion claimed to have the unique solution. Almost all, moreover, demanded exclusive belief, and stipulated the existence of an all-powerful *external* force. They urged on their devotees prayer, chanting, or meditation, in other words, a constant flow of energy from the individual toward the outside source of power. Ross told Van Rellin that he, instead, had come to believe that every person could find God within himself, and that if all this energy were turned inward, man could develop inside himself the power for good or evil. The simplicity of the concept shocked Ross once he had stated it. Yet he realized it had been taking shape all this time: his awareness of the inner potential to create your own heaven or hell.

One night after Ross got home from Van Rellin's he and Stephanie decided to attend a meeting of Students for a Democratic Society at UCLA. They had talked a great deal about "the Movement"; Ross was fascinated by the passionate commitment it inspired in its followers. Also, his conversations about God with Van Rellin had sharpened his own persistent curiosity about belief—what people believed in and why—and the SDS and similar groups seemed to be advocating a new

176

road to salvation. Furthermore, the people involved were his own generation, his and Stephanie's, and the revolution they were preaching might turn out to be his and Stephanie's revolution, too.

As they started for the UCLA campus, Ross realized how inconceivable it would have been for Ann to join him in any such quest. And he understood his real love for Stephanie. Once the meeting was under way, she was caught up in its drama and intense seriousness, and Ross himself was attracted beyond his expectations. They went to other meetings, and Ross found himself feeling strongly and thinking hard about subjects he had never before consciously confronted . . . in particular, the fiercely critical question of race relations. When they discussed such matters at home he was fiery in his condemnation of white oppression. But in public he always kept silent.

"Ross," Stephanie asked him one evening on their way to a meeting, "why don't you ever say anything at these meetings?"

"Do you think they'd listen?" he said.

"If you have something to say, they will."

That night Ross took the floor in the midst of an audience of long-haired students. Stephanie was struck by the fact that he handled them much as he had his Grim Reapers audience. He began his speech slowly and calmly, then suddenly burst forth with his salient points, emphasizing his words with his whole body as he moved about the group. People started shouting "Right on." When he was through, the group applauded.

On the way home he glanced at Stephanie. She was peering at him intently.

"The thing about those meetings, Stephanie, is they don't do as much good as they should."

"What are you talking about? I think we all got a lot done tonight."

"Listen, all these demonstrations and rallies—who goes to them? People who believe in all of it already."

"All right; so what?"

"Well, what about the outsiders? What about the millions of people who don't go? All these freaky demonstrations just make them hostile. If you believe blacks are equal to whites, then you go to a meeting or join a picket line, but if you don't believe, if you're a bigot or a redneck—man, those people are never even touched by those meetings. The meetings are just self-satisfying."

Van Rellin was at the door of their house. That had never happened before, and Stephanie felt herself trembling even with Ross beside her.

"That puppy of yours is like a horse," Van Rellin chuckled. "He broke loose from his leash and stole a leg of lamb right out of my kitchen. He's stuck up on the roof."

"Oh, no." Stephanie sighed.

"Don't worry, Mrs. Gortner, the reverend and I will get him," Van Rellin said.

"Reverend?" Stephanie mumbled. Ross took her hand and squeezed it.

"Where is he, on the slatted side?" Ross asked.

"Nope, just above the garage. I've got a ladder but I figured you'd like to do the climbing."

Ross left the house with Van Rellin and returned with Briar fifteen minutes later.

"Naughty Briar," Stephanie said to him. The oafish dog put his large paws on her lap. She petted his head for a moment and watched Ross stop at the bathroom to wash his hands.

"What's this 'reverend' thing?" she shouted over the sound of the running water. "Isn't Mr. and Mrs. enough of a put-on?"

Ross came out of the bathroom with a towel in his hands. "It's no put-on. It's just a little far out, that's all."

"You mean it's true?" Stephanie asked.

Ross sat down next to her and began to wrestle with Briar.

"Hey, come on. What is all this?" Stephanie insisted. Ross pushed Briar aside.

"I was an ordained minister. I guess I still am, although I haven't set foot in a church since I was fourteen."

"You were a minister at fourteen?" Stephanie was aghast.

"I was washed up at fourteen. I started preaching at four," Ross said earnestly.

"Is that some kind of joke?"

"It's true. I was famous; made the headlines for years."

"Are you *serious?*" she asked.

"I've never been more serious. I just never mentioned it— well, I guess I thought it was too far out. It lost its usefulness," he said.

"Where are these headlines?" she challenged him.

"In a trunk. At my father's house. He's a Pentecostal minister. My mother too. . . . I could get the newspaper clippings if you don't believe me," Ross went on.

"Call him," Stephanie dared.

Ross sat motionless next to her. "I haven't seen him in years. But maybe I will call him." He got up and walked to the wall phone in the kitchen.

"Hey," Stephanie shouted. "What's your father's name?"

"Reverend Vernon Gortner. I'm Marjoe," Ross called back.

"You're what?" she asked, following him to the kitchen.

"Marjoe. M-A-R-J-O-E."

The operator got on the line and placed the long-distance call. Stephanie watched Ross as his face darkened.

MARJOE RETURNS

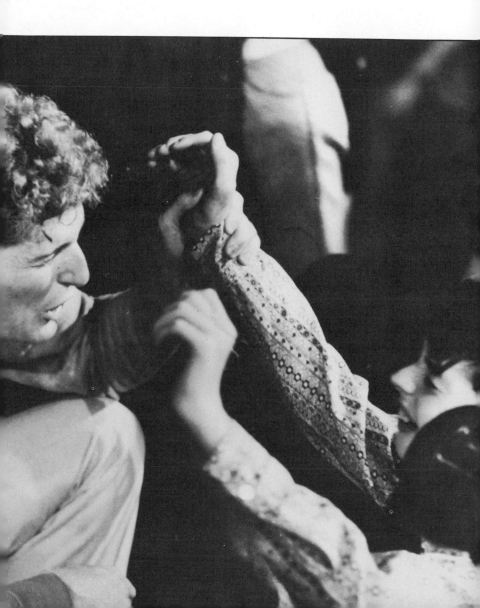

CHAPTER 9

"I'm divorced," Ross was saying into the phone. Stephanie hung on his words, unsure that what she was hearing was true. He sounded natural and friendly.

"Ginny's with Ann. I didn't call to talk to you about that, Dad. No. I'd like the trunk with all the clippings in it." Ross glanced anxiously at Stephanie, hoping it wasn't all too much at one time.

"I think they *belong* to me," he countered into the receiver. "Anyway, there's somebody I want to show them to. Yes, I remarried." There was a long pause while he stared into the phone and rolled his eyes.

"Next weekend," he finally said. "I'll bring Ginny and Stephanie." Then he hung up.

"Are you angry?" he asked her.

"I don't understand any of it," she said limply.

"I'll try to explain, but it's a pretty weird story."

"That was a pretty weird phone call," Stephanie said. She went to the stove and put up a pot of coffee, while Ross told her bits and pieces of his life.

"And now you're divorced?" she asked.

"No, I'm only separated. But then again, you and I aren't really married," he reminded her.

"Why didn't you tell me about Ann?" Stephanie asked.

"Because my marriage to Ann was a mistake, and I don't like making mistakes. Mom-Marge wanted a perfect child. I wanted to be a perfect adult and I botched that up when I was only sixteen."

"It was a child's mistake. You can still be a perfect adult," Stephanie offered. They smiled at each other and sat quietly for many minutes.

"Do you really want to be perfect?" Stephanie finally asked. Marge's words echoed back to him. "I just want to do my best," he said.

The following weekend they picked Ginny up at Ann's and drove north to Oakland. While Ginny played in the back of the bus Ross and Stephanie smoked a joint and sang songs. A short way past the Esalen Institute they found a deserted beach and all of them went skinny-dipping. Further north they stopped at a tiny Mexican shop and bought the little girl an orange fiesta dress. In Stephanie's excitement she forgot they would eventually be meeting the Reverend Vernon Gortner.

"Why did you have to tell him we were married?" she asked when they finally reached Oakland.

"Vernon never would have let me bring you to his house, let alone stay overnight, if he didn't think we were married."

The allegedly puritanical Vernon was busy closing Narver Gortner's house, where he had been living since Narver's death. When Stephanie was introduced, he spent fifteen minutes being very charming, then he got right down to business with Ross. Father and son stepped aside for a moment and Ross asked Stephanie to take Ginny into Berkeley so that he and his father could be alone.

"Why do I have to leave?" she whispered.

"Because he doesn't want to give me the trunk, or anything else here that belongs to me. I think he may want to *sell* it to me."

"Cheapskate," Stephanie said. "Don't give him a penny."

When Stephanie arrived in Berkeley with Ginny, she realized she herself didn't have a penny left. The rest of her money was in the Volkswagen at Narver's house. After half an hour of wandering around in the streets, Ginny was tired and wanted to rest. Stephanie tried to find a place to sit down, preferably someplace free. Just outside the gates of the university, Stephanie spotted an old school bus loading long-hairs for a bus ride up and down Telegraph Avenue. The bus was painted Day-Glo colors and had two loudspeakers attached to the top. Although Stephanie had no idea what the purpose of the ride was or who was taking it, she found Ginny a window seat and settled back to view the sights of Berkeley.

By the time they got off the bus Ginny was bored and hungry. The streets were lined with food stands, hot dog vendors, and little restaurants. Ginny couldn't understand why she couldn't eat. Stephanie guiltily eyed the hippie panhandlers up and down the street.

"Ginny, see those men asking for money?"

Ginny nodded. "Those men." She pointed.

"Right. Well, if you ask some nice man and woman for a quarter like they're doing, we'll be able to buy you a hot dog."

Ginny went down the street and returned in a few minutes with a handful of change. Stephanie bought her a hot dog and watched her wolf it down happily.

Two hours later they were back in Oakland. Ross had loaded the bus with his possessions. Vernon stood to the side, arms folded across his chest, not looking very happy.

"Where'd you go?" Ross asked.

"I took Ginny on a bus ride through Berkeley. How did it go with your father?"

"Not good. I don't think we should stay here."

He and Stephanie said good-bye to Vernon and drove off to the forest. Ross was feeling the familiar sense of frustration he always experienced when talking to Vernon. He had tried to discuss money honestly with his father, but Vernon feinted, dodged, backed away. Ross then tried discussing God, seriously anxious to know Vernon's real beliefs, but although Ross had changed, Vernon had not. Trying to put the incident out of his mind, he pitched the tent and they camped out that night.

The next day Ross decided to visit Marge, who wasn't very happy to see the threesome pull up in front of her house. Her first comments were about Ginny's Mexican dress, which she considered hideous. Then she knelt beside her granddaughter and tried to get pally.

"What have you been doing, Ginny?" she asked.

"We went naked swimming," Ginny told her excitedly.

Marge turned white while Stephanie and Ross complemented her with bright red.

"And what else?" Marge persisted calmly.

"Stephanie took me on a bus ride with hippies. Then I asked a man for money to buy a hot dog. Stephanie has no money," Ginny explained.

That same night Ross displayed his legacy to Stephanie. There was a twenty-six-inch pulpit, a tree stump, a dozen record albums, and piles of newspaper clippings. Stephanie began to read each clipping.

"Do you realize how incredible this is?" she asked, with a stunned look.

"Yes, that's what they said when it happened."

"But do you realize the power you had?" she insisted.

"I was doing what my parents told me to do. But I think I'll show it all to Max Van Rellin tomorrow. He'll get a kick out of it."

The next day, Mr. Denke hurried out of the Innes stockroom laden with a half-dozen boxes. He laid them at the feet of a plump woman. Another eight boxes were already piled around her chair. Ross busied himself nearby in order to eavesdrop.

"This pair, madam, has just been unpacked. I'm sure . . ."

"No bows."

Denke agreed. "Then this—fine calf, an elegant shoe."

"Calf wears poorly."

189

"And this one, madam?" Denke begged her. She curled her upper lip as though she smelled something foul. Denke opened still another box. The woman fingered the shoe with great curiosity and squinted up at the neon fixtures.

"Bad lighting for true color," she told Denke. He escorted her to the door, where she could examine the shoe in daylight. Back at the chair, he slipped the shoes on her pudgy feet.

"The vamp—is it hand sewn?" she asked.

"I believe so, madam," Denke answered.

The woman stood and walked to a mirror, pointing her toes and moving her feet in circles.

"Is the shank joined with glue or sewn?" she asked. Denke couldn't contain himself. He approached her very sweetly and began brushing imaginary lint off her shoulder. The woman's eyes crossed as she looked down at her shoulder in horror.

"Madam," Denke asked in a low voice, "could *you* pass such an inspection?"

Ross rushed to the stairway leading to the basement, grabbed five boxes of shoes, and started down the steep steps, laughing aloud. In an instant the steps were no longer beneath his feet and his stomach was dropping with a sickening plunge. The boxes flew out in front of him before they fell. He saw the ceiling pass and felt the hard smack of the steps on his calves, his buttocks, and finally his injured vertebrae.

When he first lay in bed Stephanie rushed around him frantically, as if her speed would somehow ease his pain. He patted the bed and insisted she sit beside him quietly.

"A couple of months," he groaned. "I don't think I can lie here for a couple of months."

190

"We could put the bed on wheels and I could roll you up and down the Strip."

"Very funny. What'll we do for money?"

"You'll get disability, won't you?" she asked distractedly, twirling her hair.

"Yeah, but that won't keep us very long. And I can forget about the Grim Reapers too."

"That's no great loss, I'm afraid."

"Well, we might as well make the best of it."

Stephanie sighed and got into bed.

The first day Van Rellin came up to the house to visit Ross, Stephanie made a huge bowl of chocolate mousse and the two men sat in the bedroom eating from large parfait glasses and trading newspaper clippings from the trunk.

"Ever think about going back?" Van Rellin asked. "Like the 'Miracle Adult'?"

Ross answered him seriously. "Yes. I've been thinking about it quite a lot lately."

A few days later Van Rellin came to the house with a large leather portfolio.

"This way you can make some order out of those newspaper clippings," he offered.

It had been a hot summer and they had been in the house for months. When Ross was sufficiently healed, Van Rellin suggested that he and Stephanie take a vacation. Van Rellin owned a 160-acre site near Palm Springs that was perfect for camping. They put the dogs and equipment in Ross's Volkswagen bus and set out for the desert. At night they lay huddled in blankets watching the stars.

Less than a month later Ross was dialing a phone number he had never expected to dial again.

"Brother Lucas?" he said into the phone. "This is Marjoe Gortner." Stephanie listened apprehensively as he talked.

"Going to school. Growing up, I guess. Yes, I'm married. Thank you. . . . Brother Lucas, I'm going back on the road again and I'll be in San Antonio in about a week. In two weeks? Yes, my wife and I would love it. Yes. Yes. Well, regards to Sister Lucas too. I'll see you on the fourteenth, then."

He hung up the phone. Stephanie was shaking with excitement.

"What did he say?" she asked.

"Mrs. Gortner, get yourself ready. We're starting on the gospel circuit in a week! Hallelujah!"

"Ross?" Van Rellin was calling from the open door. "Are you there?" Ross left the bedroom and met Van Rellin at the doorway.

"Hi, come on in," he told the old man.

"I have something for you to go out on the road with." Van Rellin fished around in his pocket, produced a check, and handed it to Ross.

"Thanks, but I can't take a hundred dollars from you."

"How you going to get to Texas without any cash? You'll give it back, if you want. When you have it. I'll be around." He winked.

Stephanie and Ross cashed the check and went straight to a small beauty parlor on Fairfax Avenue. It was not an especially stylish place and Stephanie couldn't understand what they were doing there.

Ross tried to explain. "These people have got to accept us for them to listen."

"Does that mean we have to look like them?"

"At least we shouldn't look different from them."

The hairdresser experimented with Stephanie's long hair. They finally compromised by pinning it up in an old-fashioned braided knot.

On the way home Ross brought up what he knew would be a painful topic.

"Do you have any idea of what you want to do with Thruppence and Briar?"

"Those people don't like dogs either?"

"Dogs have nothing to do with it. We've got to be a respectable young couple. We'll be living in motels and hotels. The dogs just don't fit in."

"I hope *I* fit in."

The following day they took the two dogs out to a ranch just north of the city, and while Stephanie waited morosely in the car, Ross gave them away to the owner.

Stephanie stored all her slacks and jeans in cartons while Ross got together his wardrobe of suits and ties. Just before leaving the city he had his hair clipped short. Early on a hazy Los Angeles morning they piled into the Volkswagen bus and headed for San Antonio. Along the rear bumper he had placed two stickers he had found in the trunk along with the newspaper clippings. They read "See Marjoe—The Miracle Child."

They reached San Antonio just before the stores closed and rushed to Sears Roebuck to buy Stephanie three very correct dresses. She giggled as she tried them on but Ross was deadly serious about what they were doing.

"Another thing, Stephanie," he told her on their way to Lucas's church. "My name is Marjoe now. Don't slip and call me Ross." She sat next to him silently repeating the name over and over again.

Lucas was a man in his late fifties. He had started his ministry more than thirty years before, in the wake of the Depression, with a mission where he fed and tended hungry and broken people. As the years passed the mission disappeared and a succession of larger churches took its place. By 1968 Lucas had built a huge house of worship on the edge of his own private lake. Two hundred feet away stood a colonial house, hidden by a grove of trees.

Lucas was delighted to see Marjoe grown up and hugged the young couple warmly at the door. Sister Lucas was in the dining room, where the welcoming dinner she had prepared was waiting for them.

"This is quite a layout, Brother Lucas," Marjoe told him. "The church right next to the house . . ."

"And picnic grounds too," Sister Lucas said. She was a tall, skinny woman, with a narrow nose ending in a bulbous stub.

"Tomorrow the youngsters from the church are having a picnic and some boating. You'll join us, won't you?"

"Sure. Delighted," Marjoe said.

He grinned at Stephanie. She shifted her weight from side to side and nodded with apparent enthusiasm. Glancing down, Marjoe saw that her dress was riding up above her knees. Casually, he spread the tablecloth over her legs.

"We worked a lot of years for all this," Lucas said, "but there's nothing as good as the old days with the mission. That was way before your time, but believe me, it gave a man real satisfaction. This is just a business now."

Sister Lucas flared up at him. "Nonsense. We're doing the Lord's work for five times as many people. And more deserving people too."

"Well, every man's satisfied by his own," Lucas told them. They all nodded in agreement.

"Your own thing," Stephanie piped in.

"Beg pardon?" Sister Lucas said.

"Do your own thing. The kids say it," Stephanie offered happily. Marjoe nudged her foot under the table and she stared quietly at her plate.

"The youngsters are ungodly creatures these days," Sister Lucas said sternly. Her husband swallowed a mouthful of food and changed the subject.

"What are you gonna preach on tomorrow, Marjoe?" he asked.

"I have a couple of new things worked out," Marjoe told

him. "God has given me a great new ministry that is going to be a blessing to everyone."

Early the next morning Stephanie and Marjoe left the small motel the Lucases had put them in and went into San Antonio.

"You need stockings, for one thing," Marjoe told her. "It's a small, small sacrifice for helping to change and enlighten the world."

They were sitting at a long redwood picnic table next to the lake. On either side of them a dozen children sat munching fried chicken.

"Do we all go to Hell if we're bad, Brother Marjoe?" a little girl asked.

Stephanie scowled at him.

"Yes, that's right. Jesus is the way to heaven, sweetheart," he said emphatically.

"What about the Chinese? Do they believe in Jesus?" another asked.

"Some of them do," Marjoe said.

"And the ones that don't—they go to Hell?"

Marjoe paused a long time. He answered without looking at Stephanie.

"That's right," he said. "You've got to love Jesus to be saved."

"Hallelujah," a little boy sang out.

"That's horrible!" Stephanie said to him in the motel. "It's really horrible, and dishonest too."

196

"Look, Stephanie, I can't change the whole religion. I have to say some things like that at times."

"You told all those little children everybody else in the world was going to wind up in Hell!" she shouted.

"That's what they're taught and that's what they believe. Did you expect to rewrite the Scriptures out here?"

"No. But I didn't expect you to lie."

"Then keep quiet and I'll do the talking. You'll feel better after the sermon tonight."

The church was packed. Behind the pulpit there was a row of leather chairs in which the Lucases sat with Marjoe and Stephanie. A choir sang a hymn from the balcony on their left. Reverend Lucas stepped up to the pulpit. Stephanie listened intently while she watched the faces in the audience.

". . . a very special guest," Lucas was saying. "The older members will remember him when he was only a little child, anointed by the Lord at the age of four to carry His word to us. And now Marjoe is back along with a lovely wife, whom I'd like to introduce to you first. Sister Gortner." Lucas beckoned Stephanie to the microphone. "Welcome to church."

She shot Marjoe a quick look and wobbled up to the pulpit and microphone. Lucas stepped aside.

"Thank you, Brother Lucas," she mumbled.

"Speak right into the microphone," he whispered.

"Thank you, Brother Lucas." Her voice echoed hollowly over the speakers. She turned to look at Marjoe behind her, hoping he would signal her or come up to the microphone and get her out of there. Marjoe had his eyes tightly closed and he was pinching the bridge of his nose with his right hand.

"I just want to say . . ." Stephanie stammered, "that it's really far out being here."

Marjoe had been at the microphone only five minutes when Lucas began to look worried.

"It was Jesus who said death and killing was a sin. It was Jesus who taught us to love all mankind. It was Jesus who gave of Himself so freely so that we might live in His divine grace and follow Him. Jesus. Think of that now, I ask you. Not a love for one man excluding others but a love for all men! And He who gave of Himself, what do we give Him? Our love? And His words? Do we ignore His words with war and death? No matter what the cause? Did Jesus justify death and destruction in Southeast Asia? I'll tell you, because he says it now, in his words. . . ."

Lucas sat next to Stephanie, watching his congregation grow more and more obviously disgruntled and hostile.

"Sister Gortner," he said to her quietly, "when will Brother Marjoe preach on the blood?"

"He preaches *against* the blood," she said proudly. Lucas was horrified.

"Sister Gortner, against the blood of our Lord?"

Lucas sat behind the desk in his study. The church had emptied an hour before.

"Marjoe, this is the worst offering we've received from the Lord in years. I don't think there's fifty dollars here." He hit the money with the back of his hand.

"I can't understand it, Brother Lucas."

"I can." Lucas took a sip of bourbon. "Where's all that fire you used to have? What's all this peace and love nonsense have to do with church?"

Marjoe shook his head. "We'll try another sermon tomorrow."

"I'd prefer not, Marjoe. I hate to ask you this but I think one night is enough. My people don't understand. Your own wife doesn't seem to understand either," Lucas said.

Marjoe left Lucas re-counting the money for the third time. Stephanie sat waiting in the bus.

"What happened?" she asked.

"Nothing much. Let's go get something to eat."

"Listen, there's some people in that car waiting to talk with you." Marjoe squinted in the darkness and saw a car parked under the trees by the picnic area. There were two people sitting in the front seat. He told Stephanie to wait where she was and he approached the waiting strangers apprehensively. A tall, balding man got out of the driver's seat.

"Brother Marjoe?" he said in the darkness.

"Yes. What can I do for you?"

"My name's Brookfield. Reverend Charles Brookfield." He extended his hand and shook Marjoe's. Marjoe felt his muscles relax.

"You had a hard time up there tonight," Brookfield said.

"You didn't like the sermon, I guess."

"No; on the contrary. I thought it was one of the best I've heard. A true interpretation of God's word."

"Well, thank you. It's good to hear."

"I heard you when you were a little boy too. I didn't have a ministry then; I was just an accountant. But you were terrific as a child."

Marjoe thanked him again.

"This is really an invitation. We have a church in Kokomo, Indiana. My wife and I." He pointed to the car, where a woman smiled and waved.

"We'd like you to preach in our church."

"I'd love to, of course. But I didn't seem to hit a jackpot on offerings tonight."

"That's a chance I'll take. I'd like to give you an advance to help you get to Kokomo. Can you make it in two weeks, let's say?"

"I can make it in a week, also," Marjoe offered. Brookfield smiled.

"A week then." He handed him a card with his address and said good-bye. Marjoe went back to his bus and climbed up next to Stephanie. He kissed her.

"What happened?" she asked.

"I've got another job! Can you believe it?" Stephanie jumped up and down in the seat as he told her the details.

"See, I told you it would work. I just knew it."

Marjoe yelled back toward Brother Lucas's church.

"Thank you, Jeeesus!"

During the next week they learned how fast word travels on the Hallelujah Trail. Lucas had phoned ahead to Marjoe's next-scheduled meeting in New Orleans. He told the minister there that Marjoe was preaching revolution instead of revelation, and the minister summarily canceled Marjoe's booking. Meanwhile Stephanie and Marjoe headed for New York, where they spent the week with a friend of Stephanie's. Marjoe had a valid credit card for their meals, but he had no idea how they would get to Kokomo until Stephanie improbably produced several rolls of dimes she had been saving ever since her days as a waitress in L.A. They used the dimes to make the long trip west.

The Brookfields' church was a modest white building in a small suburb of Kokomo.

"You know, Marjoe," Brookfield said, "I can appreciate what you're trying to do. I feel deeply for your ideals. But the people of the church can't be rushed into anything. Not even in the name of Jesus. So be patient, and . . . go a little slow with them."

"You're probably right. The Lord didn't bless me with more than fifty dollars in San Antonio. But I'd still like to try."

"Listen, Marjoe, you probably know evangelism better than I do. You preach whatever you want. My church is open to you. And no matter how the congregation reacts, I promise you two full weeks. I'll even guarantee you a minimum."

Marjoe thanked Brookfield for his generosity and went back to the motel to study and write his sermons. He and Stephanie dressed for the meeting without speaking. On the way to the church, Stephanie broke the silence.

"What if they hate it again?" she said.

"Brookfield doesn't seem to mind."

"But you do, don't you? You're worried."

"I don't like failure. I feel like I'm *disappointing* those people. They're not getting what they want."

"What they want isn't good for them," Stephanie said.

"Nonsense! What they want to hear is what they've heard all their lives. What they want is a good time, a moving experience. Stephanie, these people don't just *go* to church; they say, 'Let's *have* church!' like let's have a party."

"Teach them something," said Stephanie.

Reverend Brookfield was charming in the pulpit and it was obvious that his congregation liked him. He introduced Marjoe in a short, low-keyed speech. He told the parishioners that Marjoe had something important to say, a new, young interpretation of the Word. He told them he agreed with Marjoe, fully, and he hoped they would take Marjoe's message to their hearts.

The congregation sat stoically in their seats as Marjoe walked to the pulpit. Throughout his sermon they sat immobile, never once responding with "Hallelujah" or "Amen." When he finished, he didn't even bother to take an offering.

Brookfield suggested the offering to the congregation, encouraged them to give generously. Ushers slowly passed a tray around while Marjoe sat glumly at the back of the stage. He heard the noisy clink of quarters plopping into the collection tray as it was passed down the rows. He was furiously angry with himself. Brookfield had made a mistake in asking him to come to Kokomo. He was a failure at what he knew best. He was ending up a failure.

Marjoe and Stephanie excused themselves from dinner and retreated to the motel. He stretched out on the soft, bumpy bed and closed his eyes.

"I disappointed them."

"You didn't disappoint me," she told him.

"Tomorrow will be better. Tomorrow has to be different."

"How different?"

"One night, just one night, I've got to show them I can give them what they want. Then the rest doesn't matter. . . ."

"What they want?" Stephanie began to sound panicky. "What are you going to do?"

"An old one, in the old way."

"No—please don't. Don't lie to them."

He leaned on his elbow and looked into her eyes. He took off her glasses, kissed her, and smiled.

"I'm an entertainer," he said. Stephanie began to shake her head. "Listen carefully. I'm an entertainer for the Lord. I'm an evangelist, not a priest or a holy man. These people come to hear me to forget their miseries for a while and I've got to give them their money's worth."

Stephanie turned off the overhead light. They lay still in the darkness, listening to the cars whoosh by on the highway outside. She thought he had fallen asleep with his clothes on when she spoke aloud.

"What ever became of Ross Gortner?"

He tried again the following night. Brookfield again gave him a rousing introduction and Marjoe started his sermon with confidence, but in less than ten minutes he was thoroughly deflated. The congregation sat in their seats like wooden dolls. Brookfield's and Stephanie's were the only voices crying "Hallelujah" and "Amen." He slogged through the rest of the sermon, and when it was over he scarcely had energy enough to ask for an offering. A few handfuls of change were thrown in the baskets. Stubbornly, but with less and less conviction, he attempted to preach his "social gospel" for two more nights. At his last meeting the congregation had thinned to a dozen people. There could be no thought of continuing.

When Stephanie told him she wanted to leave, he was not surprised. They both knew a decision had to be made, and Marjoe was determined that Stephanie could not, must not, have a hand in that decision.

Brookfield was kind about lending him the money for her plane fare. Early the next evening Marjoe drove her to the airport, helped her with the luggage, waited by her side until it was time to board the plane, and kissed her without looking into her eyes. He thought about her on the ride back to the motel, during the time he spent preparing a new sermon, and up to the moment when Brookfield turned the microphone over to him. Then he was conscious only of the energy surging in his veins, and the gospel, and the people.

"I've come before you to talk about Hell. Hell is a place . . ." he began.

Stephanie spoke to him a week later from a friend's apartment in New York. Brookfield had asked him to stay an extra week, after which he had two more weeks booked with an old-timer he knew in Tulsa. He promised to call from Oklahoma and arrange to see her. When his call from Tulsa was two days late, Stephanie began phoning the state trooper stations along the route from Kokomo to Tulsa. No accident involving Marjoe had been reported, however, and she thought for a while he had vanished from her life.

But Marjoe finally called, to say that he would join her in New York in two weeks' time. He had spent the preceding days entirely alone, weighing his next step, analyzing his motives, trying to make sure that he was doing the right thing before going on to his meeting in Tulsa. The process of reaching a decision turned out to require a reappraisal of everything he had learned since he was a child.

The congregations had not changed since he first stood behind his twenty-six-inch pulpit and forecast an eternity in Hell. On the Pentecostal circuit there were still no ears to take in the "social gospel." The parishioners did not come to church to hear what man can do to help the world become a better place. If they were better educated now, their education had not yet affected their beliefs. Marjoe was no longer the Miracle Child who had thrilled and inspired millions, but the congregations on the Hallelujah Trail had not outgrown their primal need. His sermons on Hell at Brookfield's church were as successful as any evangelist could hope for, and as word got out that he finally had something to say, attendance increased spectacularly . . . along with the offerings.

The lesson was unmistakable. He was in *their* church, their spiritual refuge, and they would pay only for what they wanted to hear: the gospel as their forebears had heard it for generations.

In a sense, Marjoe's decision made itself. He could not deny the facts or their meaning. He could only try to be a better evangelist, and hope that somewhere in his sermons people would discover something to make them happier, better, kinder than before.

By the time he reached Tulsa he knew what he was doing and why. Brookfield had phoned ahead with a recommendation. The word was out. The all-time-great child evangelist was back and preaching the blood as no one had in years.

Purposely he did not arrive at the church until just before he was to speak. The minister and the deacons shook his hand excitedly when he finally entered the auditorium and took a seat on the stage. The minister introduced him briefly, concluding with ". . . welcome to the Reverend Marjoe Gortner!"

Marjoe walked slowly to the microphone and took it off the pulpit, stretching the long cable out behind him.

He began quietly. He whispered into the microphone. "The Holy Ghost is here. The Holy Ghost is in this church. I know it. I feel it. Somebody's going to get touched."

Then he exploded.

"Hallelujah, I said, I said Hallelujah. The Lord's in here, I feel it, the Lord is here."

"Amen, Amen!"

"And we're gonna praise him. Say Glory!"

"Glory!"

"And we're gonna love him. Say Hallelujah!"

206

"Hallelujah!"

"I've been high riding and low sliding. Busting heads and dropping reds! Slashing tires and setting fires! Kickin' in doors and banging whores! Shooting and looting! Then I met a Man who was hung up for my hang-ups. Jesus said, 'If I'll be lifted up I'll draw all men to me!' Say Thank you, Jesus! Amen. Say Thank you, Jesus!"

"Hallelujah!"

"Hallelujah!"

"I want those of you who feel Jesus, who *really feel* Jesus, to come up here. Come right on up and form a line to your left, 'cause I feel the spirit rising in me. I feel it. Hallelujah!"

A line formed. Three ushers stood near Marjoe. He grabbed the head of the woman first in line, exerting pressure on her skull. Sweat covered her face, burned her eyes.

"Say Thank you, Jesus!"

But the woman was unable to speak. Her head rolled backward, spasms started in her chest, seized her entire body. The spirit filled her, and the gift of tongues poured from her mouth. She became dead weight in the ushers' arms, and expertly they dipped her backward and out of the way of the oncoming people. She lay unconscious on the floor, and someone covered her legs with a cloth. Marjoe had already moved on, to another woman, this one sturdy and less transported. He blessed her, asked her to thank Jesus, and pushed her out of his way. A man came up to him, shirt drenched dark blue with sweat, face flushed bright red. Marjoe reached his left hand around to the back of the man's head, driving his fingers deep into the throbbing scalp. His right hand pushed flat against the man's chest.

207

"I feel the Holy Ghost moving in you!" Marjoe began. The man tried to fall, but Marjoe didn't want him down yet.

"Say Thank you, Jesus!"

"ThaaankyouuJesus!" the man babbled.

"Shout it! Shout! Thank you, Jesus!"

The man's breath came short. He moaned. He could no longer stand. They let him drop. Two women farther out in the crowd collapsed in psychic sympathy. Their hands fluttered at their sides. In the last row a man stood with his hands above him, waiting to soar skyward like Superman. His throat filled with guttural noises and saliva sputtered from his mouth.

The bills came sailing in, flying through the air, thrown at the altar, laid at Marjoe's feet. The minister stood in awe at the back of the stage.

"Billy Sunday," he mumbled to Marjoe when it was all over.

The minister in Tulsa begged him to stay on an extra week, but Marjoe was determined to get to Stephanie. He left his Volkswagen bus parked at the airport and grabbed the first flight out.

Stephanie was waiting in her friend's apartment. When he finally walked in the door, she felt awkward and embarrassed. They kissed each other lightly and stood there grinning.

Later that night, as they were having dinner, Marjoe began to tell her about the new meetings, and his rediscovered vocation. She listened in silence.

"I'm glad, I guess." She parceled out the words reluctantly.

"Stephanie, I'm good at it," he said.

"I know." She paused nervously, playing with her napkin.

Her face felt flushed and feverish. "Will I only see you week-ends?"

"Unless you want to come back with me."

"Quit it, Ross. Let's go back to L.A."

"I don't want to quit it. I'm good at it, and I may even do some good." He grinned at her tenderly. "And it's in my blood now. Maybe I'm becoming addicted."

When the news spread that he was back for good, the churches started competing for him. Amazingly, before very long he began to get invitations from black congregations too. This was a great compliment. Not many white preachers were invited to preach in black churches. They seemed awkward and out of tune with the vibrant and joyous temper of the meetings. At the same time, Marjoe had come to recognize certain un-pleasant traits in the all-white congregations he was now en-countering. They tended to sniff out scandal, even where none existed. Their ministers' private lives were under constant scrutiny, and no lapse was ever forgiven. When they were in church they were militant in their virtue, but as soon as the church doors closed behind them they were likely to do as they pleased. But the blacks, Marjoe felt, were more consistent about their religion. If you slipped and sinned, well, it was only human and church was the place to be absolved. He admired this wholeness and sincerity, and the black congregations sensed his approval. They responded to him even more readily than the whites, and he felt they might even remember his sermons when they went home. Perhaps they were the people he could really reach as an evangelist.

Eventually Marjoe was preaching in many more black churches than white. These meetings began somewhat later, usually about eight o'clock. And they could go on all night. The parishioners were there to have fun. They were there to have church.

Marjoe would arrive at the meeting a half hour after it began. He would use the rear entrance of the church and wait upstairs with the minister while one of the deacons ran the meeting downstairs. They began with gospel hymns. The people wanted to let *loose,* and music was the ideal way to release their tensions. Secluded in the office upstairs, Marjoe could hear them singing for nearly an hour, the voices and harmonies enthralling, professional. Then the deacon would call on those who wanted to testify, and one by one they would come up to the microphone to tell their brothers and sisters what God had done for them. The miracles He had worked were as varied as they were numerous. He had given them new automobiles, found them jobs, cured their illnesses, and saved their children from drug addiction. When the testifying was over, the congregation was again wound tight, waiting to be released by the evangelist.

The minister would leave the office and walk onto the stage. His congregation would grow quiet as he talked about the church and its programs. He would take several offerings to support the programs, and then he would begin to build to the curly-haired white man waiting in the wings.

"I can *feeel* it!" he shouted, "We're having church to-*night!* I just left Brother Marjoe, and you're all gonna get a chance to meet this boy in a few minutes. But first we need a little song to get the spirit moving again."

The choir began to sing. People started clapping. Some of them moved down the aisles, dancing. Marjoe slipped onto the stage and began to clap and dance with them. He watched their faces, hopeful and joyous. He felt his energy rising to match theirs.

"Tonight we are privileged to have in our midst a man who is called of God! This boy's been a minister since he was four years old!"

The congregation answered readily. "Whooo!"

"I want you all to honor him tonight! Don't be deceived by his skin. His skin may be white but his soul is black! His name is Marjoe Gortner!"

There was a sprinkling of applause as Marjoe walked up to the pulpit. He began to speak slowly, almost drawling his words.

"In-case-you-haven't-detected-it, *the Holy Ghost is here!*"

"Yes!"

"Hallelujah!"

He waved his hand over them as if casting a spell.

"I feel a chill running up and down my spine!"

Someone from the audience yelled out, "He's got the *stuff!*"

"I didn't come out here tonight to talk to you or just preach a sermon. I came out here tonight to let God move! There are some preachers today that can talk a lot, but all they've got is the Holy Boast. I've come to preach about the Holy *Ghost!*"

"Hallelujah!"

211

"Now I want all of you to do something for me. I want everyone to stand. That's right, stand right up. Now take the hands of the person right next to you. Both hands, now."

The congregation was on its feet, holding each other, smiling up at the man on the stage.

"Now repeat after me! 'I am for you!' "

"I am for you!"

"I love you!"

"I love you!"

"And by this all men shall know that we are disciples and have loved one to another!"

"Amen!"

"Now raise your hands and praise the Lord!"

A sea of hands waved back and forth through the air, curling, pulsating. Marjoe took the microphone out of its stand and jumped off the front of the stage. He spoke in tongues.

"Ada mana non sacaria!"

The usherettes sitting in the first three rows, all dressed in white, moved forward and began to clap. Little children stood in the aisles to get a better view.

"Now I want to see everyone here tonight who's got their Bible. I believe when you come to church you've got to have a Bible!"

The congregation chorused their answer at the end of every sentence. "Hallelujah! Yes!"

"Now take those Bibles and hold them over your head!"

Hundreds of black books were in the air.

Marjoe held his own hand over his head.

"Wave it! Wave it! Do you know this is our most priceless possession next to salvation? The Word of God!"

"Amen!"

"God has said in the Bible, 'Thy word have I hid in my heart that I might not sin against thee.' Now repeat that!

"When you come to church bring your Bible! Shame on you that can't raise a Bible over your head!"

He began to walk down the aisles, scolding them. They loved it. They egged him on, joined him with their shouted repetitions of his words. His body was becoming drenched in sweat.

He stopped in front of a man who was not holding a Bible.

"How can I preach to you and tell you the Word when you don't even bring your Bible? We're not here to play. We're here to pray! Read the Word! Right out of the Bible! Now everybody who has a Bible stand with me and read."

The congregation stood and read aloud with him as he walked back to the pulpit. He waited there for them to settle into their seats. After a moment the church was quiet. His body swooped forward.

"Can God deliver a dope addict?" he roared, one finger pointing toward the ceiling.

"Yes he can!" they shouted.

"Can God deliver a homosexual?"

"Yes he can!"

"Can God deliver an alcoholic?"

"Yes he can!"

He walked back down the steps of the platform, taking his time, waiting for the emotion to subside. The air was thick and warm, and at the back of the church ushers opened the windows to let fresh air wash over the crowd. A man stood in his seat and began to speak in tongues. Marjoe started to whisper into the microphone, drawing the people to him, watching them lean toward him. He continued to murmur hypnotically as they strained to hear him.

"More than nineteen centuries ago he was born in adversity and reared in obscurity. His birth was contrary to the laws of life as his death was contrary to the laws of death. In infancy he startled a king, in boyhood he puzzled the doctors. In manhood he gave his life—a ransom for many. He didn't own any cornfields or fisheries, but he could spread a table for five thousand with bread and fish enough to spare. He never walked on any soft, plush, beautiful carpets but he walked the seas of Galilee and they supported him.

"Three years he preached the gospel, during which time he never wrote a book, but all the libraries cannot contain the books that have been written about him. He never painted pictures, but the works of Raphael, Michelangelo, Leonardo da Vinci were all influenced by him. He never wrote poetry, but the works of Shakespeare, Dante, Longfellow were all influenced by him. No wonder the psalmist David cried, 'Who in heaven could be compared unto the Lord? Who among the sons of the mighty can be likened unto him?'

"Aristotle taught for forty years, Plato taught for fifty years, Socrates taught for forty years, but Jesus taught for only three years. Yet the influence of these three years transcended the combined influence of a hundred and thirty years of three

214

of the greatest men of antiquity.

"He never made claims of being a great public speaker. Caruso, that great Italian opera singer, could sing at full volume and shatter a glass tumbler a few feet away. Hitler spoke and captured millions with the power and strength of his voice. But never—never—a man spoke like this man!"

He paused and eyed the room. People sat motionless, the sound still hanging thickly in the air. In a sudden movement he leaped from the stage and landed in front of a teetering woman. His hand flashed out to touch the top of her head, and as he made contact she spun away dancing. He shouted his next words through the microphone and every syllable reverberated in their ears.

"He sp-o-ke and the water turned to wine!"

"Hallelujah!"

"He sp-o-ke and blind eyes were open!"

"Amen!"

"He sp-o-ke and the country winds subsided!"

"He sp-o-ke and the demons feared and trembled!"

"He sp-o-ke and the common people accepted him gladly!"

"He sp-o-ke and the dead came to life!"

"He sp-o-ke and the oceans supported him like a sidewalk!"

"Hallelujah!" they shouted back at him. People hugged each other.

"Don't you know Herod couldn't kill him? Satan couldn't seduce him?

"Death couldn't destroy him. And the grave couldn't hold him!"

From his back pocket he produced a bandanna and wiped

215

the sweat from his eyes. Then he leaned forward, one hand on his hip, the other bringing the microphone to his lips.

"Now let me ask all of you a ser-i-ous question. Do you know what the biggest monster of sin is? It is the *love of money!*" They laughed and shouted agreement, but Marjoe pretended they didn't believe him.

"That's right! The love of money!"

He pointed to a group of people smiling at him.

"Now don't tell me you don't love it, because I know you do!"

"You tell it!" an old man shouted.

"That's right! I see you going into a shop and trying to Jew the owner down on the price. I see you trying to get a price that you know isn't right."

"Yessirr!"

"Even good Christian folks do it, so don't shake your head no at me." No one was shaking his head; they were waiting for his next words.

"The man in the family works. He sends his wife out to work. Even the children work! If a dog and cat could speak they'd put them to work too!"

The people around him laughed and clapped.

"Now, for Jesus, for Jesus you have no money. For Jesus who loves you, you have no cash—*you robbers you!*"

He turned to the organist and gave him a signal. The congregation began to sing with him. His hoarse voice rasped over the speakers. The people danced up the aisles, tears mixed with their sweat. He sang with them until the music was over, and then he calmed them.

"Now I want all of you who want to be blessed, all of you who want me to pray for you or help you with an illness, to form a line here to my left."

Nearly a third of the five hundred people joined the line. They began to pass by him slowly as he touched their foreheads and held their hands. Some just asked for a prayer, and Marjoe clamped his eyes shut and spoke to God for them. Down the line a lady with a large white hat mumbled about a pain in her back. She'd had it three months, she murmured timidly.

"Now wait a minute!" Marjoe signaled for the congregation to be still. "Hold everything. Now here's a lady that's had a pain in her back for three months. Do you have pain right now?"

He put the microphone to her lips.

"Yes, I *do*."

"Now where is this pain? Tell the people right now."

She tried to back away.

"We're not afraid to say this out loud! God says he can heal!"

He made her pain very open, insisting that God could cure her. An usherette removed her white hat. She stood there, trusting, believing.

"Now everyone say Jesus!"

The crowd yelled "Jesus," but Marjoe was not satisfied.

"Now wait a minute! The way we *feel* God in here tonight and you can't even say 'Jesus'? Maybe we ought to all go home right now. Let me hear it! Jesus!"

The name thundered at him from five hundred throats.

"Jesus!"

217

"If you're gonna call upon the name of our Lord Jesus Christ you gotta say it with feeling! Now yell 'Jesus!' for this lady!"

"JESUS!"

He put one hand on the woman's forehead and the other on her afflicted back.

"In the name of Jesus I take authority over you! Demon of pain that's binding my sister's back, *come out! Come out, I order you!*"

The woman shrieked.

"I felt it!" Marjoe yelled into his microphone. "I don't have to pray anymore. Sister, did you feel that?"

But she was no longer standing in front of him. She was lying on the ground, hot and sweaty, but shivering with the fear and joy of the Lord.

"She is *out!*" Marjoe announced. He knelt down beside her. "Something must have happened! What happened? Where did you *go?*" he asked her.

"Yes! It happened. Yes, yes, yes! Praise God! *Praise God!*"

He helped her to her feet.

"Do you feel that pain anymore?"

She shook her head no and tried to move away, but Marjoe held fast to her.

"Now wait-a-minute! You said you *don't feel any pain at allllll?*" He punched each word into the microphone. "You said a minute ago you had a pain in your back that you had for three months and now that pain is gone? Now we have to be honest! Don't say anything that isn't true! Are you sure?"

"It's gone!" she cried.

"Now tell it true! 'Cause if it's not gone we're gonna pray again." The woman rolled her eyes back, drained of energy.

"It's gone!" she cried. "Praise the Lord! It's gone!"

The organ and choir began. People danced with each other, in and out of the prayer line. Women sat in their seats and wept. Marjoe passed among the people standing near him, lightly touching them, sensing who could be cured and who could not. He listened as they spoke into the microphone.

"Bless my house so I can pay my mortgage."

"Pray I get a job."

"Bless my children."

"Pray I get a man."

He told each one the same thing. "Claim what you want! You want a big black shiny Cadillac? You go outside and touch one of those automobiles and claim it!"

An ancient woman came up to him, her mouth open to show her toothlessness, one arm twisted tightly against her body. Her eyes met Marjoe's. She looked up to the tall white man through misty eyes filled with hope. The organ music swelled and died away as he began to talk sweetly to her.

"Sister, I see great courage and great belief in your eyes. I see a woman who feels the Holy Spirit in her."

"Amen," she answered.

"What's wrong with you, sister?"

"My arm's been twisted with arthritis for near five years."

He stooped down until their faces were only inches apart, the microphone separating them. Then he shouted at her, and she flinched from the force of the sound.

"Do you believe?"

"I do."

"Do you *believe?* Let me *hear* you!"

"I *do!*"

He threw his head back and bellowed, "DO YOU BE-LIEVE, SISTER?"

Following him, she too threw her head back, pleading, screaming, promising, *"I do believe, I do believe, I do—"*

Before she could finish, Marjoe placed one hand firmly on her shoulder, his long fingers bracing her. Smoothly tucking the microphone under his arm, he tugged at her twisted limb with his free hand, jerking it forward and up. The woman gasped. The people standing nearby in the prayer line saw it first. A short man fell to his knees, tugging at his shirt and tie as if he were suffocating. "Oh, Jesus, oh, Jesus . . ." he moaned. Marjoe lifted the once twisted arm high over the woman's head.

"Sister! *It is straight! Sister, your arm is straight!"*

In the pews they chanted praises to the Lord. The organ began again as Marjoe marched the old woman around in a circle, her arm high above her head. His shirt was drenched, clinging to his tall, thin body. An usher helped lead the crying woman back to her seat.

After forty minutes the line was finished. A deacon handed Marjoe a gray sweat shirt that he pulled on to cover his wet body. He spoke into the microphone quietly.

"God is here tonight. Surely God is blessing this ministry here tonight. If you haven't felt the Holy Ghost here tonight, then you're dead and you don't know it." He paused and

220

looked around the room, waiting for them to grow still again.

"Now all of you know that it takes money to help build the kingdom of God. I talked to you about the love of money. Well, you're going to have to love God more than you do money. You come to church and watch people get healed all night like this and you won't give one penny to God. No wonder you sit there with aches and pains and don't get healed. Maybe that's your problem. Give and it shall be given unto you. Shaken down, pressed together, and running over. All right. How many of you will give ten dollars tonight? I'd love to see ten of you give ten dollars tonight. . . ."

Once again his fame traveled like a brush fire. He started a Youth Crusade that allowed him to let his hair grow longer. He adopted Vernon's techniques with props. He carried with him grosses of bandannas stamped "Marjoe's Miracle Handkerchief" and he sold them at meetings for ten dollars each. He painted crosses on his forehead and, as he perspired, the crosses appeared and disappeared. He quoted Bob Dylan. His sermons had titles like "How Hip Is God?" And the men and women adored him, fell at his feet, showered him with money.

The first year he worked hard to perfect his gift for making people faint. It was easy enough to do by grabbing and pushing them, but that wasn't his idea. He wanted the spirit to move them, and he tried to make them collapse by jabbing his forefinger at them. It was in Detroit that he asked everyone to stand who did not feel the power of God within them. Sixteen men and women stood up. He lined them up against the far wall and, as they stood there, he preached that the sinner would stand fast in his sin but the saved would yield. Then he lifted his hand and jabbed his finger at them. Exhausted by standing, hypnotized by his voice, they fell to the floor like a row of dominoes. If he had failed he would have been laughed out of the church. But Marjoe couldn't fail with the gospel.

The black churches of the Northeast were the last to welcome him. Most black congregations had a leader who determined the group's reaction to the preacher. This leader was always a woman, and she sat in the front row dressed in white with a corsage pinned to her breast. Marjoe invariably began his sermons by preaching to her, until she finally cued the rest of the congregation to agree that this white, long-haired preacher really had the spirit.

At a meeting in the Bedford-Stuyvesant section of Brooklyn, he was the second speaker only, preceded by a black evangelist whose sermon was one of the best Marjoe had ever heard. By the time the black evangelist was through, he had spoken two hours and taken six collections. The crowd was washed out and ready to go home. There was a general groan as the pulpit was turned over to Marjoe. But he took the microphone in hand, jumped off the stage, and stood in front of the congregation leader. He preached to her and her alone for twenty minutes, pouring into her every ounce of energy he could summon. Finally she stood in her place, extended her arm full length, and lightly touched his chest. She looked him in the eye, but spoke to her congregation.

"This-white-boy-can-*preach!*" she whooped.

He did twenty more minutes and topped the other six collections with his one.

222

In 1970, after serving as technical adviser on a religious film that was being shot in Jerusalem, he drove his Corvette Stingray through the Malibu hills to a tiny caretaker's house on a large ranch. Stephanie lived there with five dogs. He told her about Europe and the Middle East, and she talked about her life in Los Angeles. They were strangers sitting on either side of a wooden table in her kitchen, sipping tea laced with honey. When the visit had run its course he promised to be back again in a few weeks.

"Will it ever be over?" she asked him. He stood by his car, glanced up at the sky and down at his feet.

"I don't know if I can get out of it."

Stephanie says she never cries. Never cried before Hugh Marjoe Ross Gortner and never cried after. But she cried when he left. Only because she realized she had lost him a long time before and because she thought she had failed him. White rabbits disappear down rabbit holes, and little girls wake up to find it was all a dream.

From the first meeting in Tulsa after his decision, Marjoe reveled in his rediscovered powers. The zeal of his congregations, the electric energy that poured along the circuit he could activate at will—flowing outward from his pulpit to his listeners and back from them to him—exhilarated him, sustained his sense of selfhood. He took pleasure in his increasing expertise. He was respected and admired throughout the evangelical world. For the first two years, the meetings were a delight.

He enjoyed, too, the excitement of living in two worlds, the

223

kick of getting away with something—perhaps an echo of his childhood flirtation with Satan, when he had—briefly—hidden away a few twenty-dollar bills. When he was in the East he spent his free time in New York, staying at the Hotel Chelsea. He played with people in the fashion world—designers, models —who were fascinated by him and his career. Then, back on the road, he damned the new styles as lures of the devil. Miniskirts were from the devil's wardrobe. Similarly, tobacco was from Satan's front lawn, but as an ordained minister, he could safely travel with an ounce of grass and never be concerned with the police. And although on the gospel trail he denounced the lusts of the flesh, there was almost always an airline stewardess waiting for him back in the motel.

He was famous. He was everything Marge and Vernon Gortner had dreamed he might be. But he was alone. And after a while he was forced to admit that the energy flow was more and more going one way only: out. The responsiveness of his congregations no longer seemed to revitalize him, recharge his batteries. Despite his greater fluency, his sharpened sense of timing, his total professional confidence, it was costing him more and more to generate the psychic force that made the meetings work. He could do it, but, as the months went by, he could do it only as an exercise of will. And when a meeting ended, he was empty, flat, worn out. In the long inner debate before going on to Tulsa, he had asked himself, "Why not?" Now the question was "Is it worth it?"

The calling was in his blood; Mom-Marge had seen to that. The money was good; Vernon had taught him how. The tempo of the life was too strong to slacken and ease off, and he wielded his power too well to face letting go of it slowly and painfully. In the end he supposed it would have to be all or nothing. But although he knew the end was bound to come, he couldn't see it yet. He went on. And it kept getting harder, and it started spoiling his taste for pleasure, and he went on, and presently nothing was any fun—on the road or off it.

On Sunday, May 24, 1971, Marjoe arrived at a church in Raleigh, North Carolina, early enough to hear the morning sermon. The parking lot was jammed with cars as he parked his bus and pushed his way through the crowds into a large modern brick building. In a rear office on the second floor the minister stood at a window overlooking the lot, proudly surveying the scene.

"Marjoe! You're early," the minister told him.

"I thought I'd stop in to hear the morning sermon."

"Perfect. I got a real humdinger for you. Today I'm going to destroy that which is sinful." He smiled, showing capped teeth.

"Nearly everything's sinful now. What are you destroying today?"

"Rock-and-roll. I got a new sermon I call 'The Devil's Symphony.' "

Marjoe wasn't sure what the minister meant.

"What are you going to do?"

"I'm gonna break the kids' records and—"

"*The kids' records?* Do you think that's right?"

"Course it's right. Is that *music* right? Those dances and writhin' and sexy movements." He motioned down to the crowds in the lot.

"My people like the idea, anyhow. I've been buildin' to it for weeks. Com'ere, look at that crowd!"

In the parking lot below Marjoe could see nearly a hundred teen-agers standing around. The trunks of most of the cars were open, and people were lifting out cartons filled with records.

"First a sermon," the minister told him, "and then I'm gonna break 'em."

While the minister preached, Marjoe sat onstage watching the congregation he would himself be preaching to that evening. Many of the young people had accompanied their parents.

"Sin is absolutely everywhere, I'm telling you!"

The minister screamed so loudly that the muscles and veins stood out in his neck.

"And they're feeding it to our children. Spoon-feeding it! Right in front of us. Glorifyin' drugs, glorifyin' revolution, glorifyin' sex. Now I'm gonna ask you, how many unwed mothers have we had in this very city in one single year? Well, I tell you. Eight thousand young girls led astray by that communistic propaganda they call rock-and-roll!

"Now, you hear me tell you Jesus speaks to you. God is in you. And many of you know it's true! Many of you sittin' out there have felt the Lord within your body. Am I right?"

There were isolated cries of "Amen" and "Hallelujah."

226

"Now you're goin' to hear me tell you the devil speaks to you too. The devil speaks to you in more ways than Jesus. You know why? Because you gotta come to Jesus and find him. But the devil's like a cockroach, squeezin' through every inch of space, invadin' our homes, our lives, the lives of our children. And he reaches our children with blasphemous rock-and-roll.

"Ever see those musicians? Hair so long we don't know if they're men or women. And what difference? I've been told from reliable sources most of 'em are faggots! And all of them are drug addicts!

"Brother Marjoe, here, will tell you this firsthand tonight. He works the miracles of God with our young people. Brother Marjoe's dedicated his life and his ministry to the little ones. Jesus anointed this boy when he was only four years old, and when Jesus anoints a child, he's tryin' to tell us something! And that something is *our children are in trouble!* And they get that trouble with indecent short skirts, with drugs, with long-haired faggots, and it's delivered right to their homes, yes, *your own homes* by the devil in disguise as rock-and-roll!

"We gonna let the devil take our children?"

"*No!*"

"We gonna let the devil warp 'em? Make 'em into drug addicts? Perverts? Revolutionaries?"

"*No!*"

"Then we're gonna send Satan straight back to Hell! Are you with me?"

"*Yes!*"

"Now bring them records up here!"

Hundreds of records were brought up to the front of the

altar. The minister seized them in a frenzy, tearing at the covers, breaking the discs over his knee, stomping on them, bending, twisting. Marjoe watched.

"It's sickness we're destroyin'!" the minister shouted.

Four men raced forward from the congregation to help their minister eradicate the evil from their children's lives. The pile of black fragments beside the altar grew taller.

In an hour, when it was over, a dozen teen-agers milled around the pile. The minister stood by the front doors, exuberantly shaking hands with his parishioners. Marjoe stood looking at the broken records.

"Brother Marjoe?"

A pretty young girl stood behind him. Three friends were with her. She smiled at him, although she was obviously distressed. Something in her manner reminded Marjoe of Stephanie. He smiled back at the group.

"Is rock-and-roll really from the devil?" she asked him.

"I listen to it and I still feel saved. But your pastor doesn't think that way," he answered.

"But is it really wrong?" she persisted. A young boy next to her stepped forward.

"Will it really make us into drug addicts?" he asked.

Marjoe tried to speak but it was impossible. Instead he continued to smile, hoping that the warmth and pity he felt could somehow be transmitted wordlessly. Then, before they could question him again, he bolted up the aisle toward the front doors.

"Brother Marjoe?" the girl called after him. "Brother Marjoe!"

228

The minister was surrounded by people congratulating him. Marjoe cut through the crowd and gripped his arm. "I have to speak to you," he whispered.

"Now? Not now," the minister said firmly.

"It has to be now. I won't be able to preach this week."

"Won't be able . . . ? Why not?"

"God is calling me on," Marjoe told him.

"Calling you on? Where?"

"Not here," Marjoe said, and walked away.

He got into the Volkswagen bus. In a few minutes, by speeding, he could reach the highway. He stopped for a red light at the corner and threw the bus into neutral. Through his rear-view mirror he could see the church, and the parking lot, and his future . . . breaking kids' records over his knee. Then he ran the red light.

When the highway was clear he made a broad U-turn and headed northeast. Ahead lay New York, where, possibly, he could get lost, and found again.

On the long drive he sang aloud to keep himself company. Mom-Marge had written the song for him twenty-three years before.

> My name is Marjoe Gortner
> I'm only four years old
> I'm coming to your town
> To shoot the devil down
> So come and go with me
> And surely you will see
> Me preach the old-time gospel
> And have a jubilee.

APPENDIX

HELL WITH THE LID OFF

Portions of the famous sermon as delivered by six-year-old Marjoe, August 27, 1950, in Muskegan, Michigan.

I stand before you with two great desires this afternoon. One is to go to Heaven myself, the other one is to take you along with me. If I do not preach as I should, what will become of me? If you do not hear as you should, what will become of you? "For how shall we escape if we neglect so great a salvation?"

As I stand before you this afternoon, my heart is very burdened. I feel there is someone here who is hearing the Gospel call for the last time. What if it is YOU, my friend? Christians, please pray that I may preach so plain this afternoon that many souls may come to Jesus, and so that I will not be responsible on the judgment day.

I announced I would preach another sermon today and I intended to, but last night God spoke to my little heart and told me to preach on "HELL." I didn't want to, but again at 4:00 this morning, God awakened me and I knew I would fail God if I didn't preach on Hell.

Luke 16:19–31—"There was a certain rich man, who was clothed in purple and fine linen, and fared sumptuously every day: And there was a certain beggar named Lazarus, who was laid at his gate full of sores. And desiring to be fed the crumbs which fell from the rich man's table; moreover the dogs came and licked his sores. And it came to pass, that when the beggar died, and was carried by the angels into Abraham's bosom; the rich man also died, and was buried. And in hell he lifted up his eyes, being in torments, and seeth Abraham afar off, and Lazarus in his bosom. And he cried and said, Father Abraham, have mercy on me, and send Lazarus, that he may dip the tip of his finger in water, and cool my tongue; for I am tormented in this flame. But Abraham said, Son, remember that thou in thy lifetime receivedest thy good things, and likewise Lazarus evil things; but now he is comforted, and thou art tormented. And beside all this, between us and you there is a great gulf fixed; so that they who would pass from hence to you cannot; neither can they pass to us, that would come from thence. Then he said, I pray thee, therefore father, that thou wouldest send him to my father's house: For I have five brethren; that he may testify unto them, lest they also come into this place of torment. Abraham saith unto him, they have Moses and the prophets; let them hear them. And he said, Nay, Father Abraham: but if one went unto them from the dead, they will repent. And he said unto him, if they hear not Moses and the prophets, neither will they be persuaded, though one rose from the dead."

This afternoon I want to give you a word picture of Hell. I say *Hell is a place of extreme bodily suffering.* In this life we do not like to bear pain. If you have a headache, you get an aspirin to relieve it. If you are very sick you call the doctor, and he may give you a shot or if you undergo an operation you take an anaesthetic. No. we do not want to bear pain. Listen to me, my friend. *In Hell you will suffer!* In Hell you will have pain and there will be no pills, medicine, doctors, or anaesthetics to relieve your pain. Let us refer to the rich man and Lazarus. The rich man being in Hell, seeth Father Abraham afar off and that old beggar so comfortable on his bosom; and the rich man cried: "I am tormented in this flame." Ah yes, he suffered in Hell.

Again, I say, Hell is a place of memory. Let us refer again to the rich man and Lazarus. Abraham said to the rich man, "Son remember." You will remember this very service, how God sent a wee six-year-old to warn you. You will remember every gospel service you were in. You will remember every gospel song you heard. Yes, you will remember every opportunity you had to repent and you would give the universe for one more chance, but it will *too late, too late!* On earth you can escape from your sins and the memory of them. You can forget your trouble by going to a show. You can forget and drown your cares by going to some amusement. Not so in *Hell.* You will remember, remember, remember.

Hell is a place of remorse! Let me tell you what remorse is. If your darling mother dies and you stand by the still form in the casket and look on that face you love and realize she will never say your name again. You haven't been the boy or girl you should have been. You wring your hands and tears stream down your face and in agony you say, "Oh Mother, if only you would open those eyes and let me tell you how much I love you. Oh Mother, if only I could have another chance." But it's too

233

late! *That is remorse!* Go on, lay all the flowers you can carry and place them on her grave. She will not know it. Listen to me boys and girls, you better treat your mothers and fathers right now. You won't always have them. Yes, in Hell, remorse over opportunities you let slip by will eat at your soul like a canker.

Hell is a place of shame. Oh, the heartbreaking agony of shame. Down here in this life you can hide the things you're ashamed of. Lots of you are guilty of the same sin you condemn in another person, but you are smart. You covered yours up. Oh yes, lots of you have done things you are ashamed of and you think it's all right. No one knows. . . . Let me tell you there's an eye watching you and He knows your sins. There's an eye that sees all the mean things you have done. Maybe your mother and father do not know what kind of a person you really are, but there's an eye watching you. All your sins are being recorded and one day they will be read out to the whole wide world. Oh the shame that will fill your soul then, and torment you for all eternity. Yes, Hell is a place of shame.

Again I say, *Hell is a place of loneliness.* A lady in my service in Grand Rapids, last week, when I asked her if she was a Christian, said, "I don't care if I do go to Hell, I'll have lots of company." Yes, she will have lots of company all right, but each person will be so taken up with his own suffering that he will have no time for her and she will feel she is all alone. Oh how terrible to be alone in Hell. I have heard my daddy tell of a great bank robbery in Brooklyn, New York, when four young men shot down two bank messengers in cold blood, and escaped with $50,000. The law was fast on their tracks and each of the four young men was apprehended in different cities. Each was tried and found guilty and all four were sentenced to die in Sing Sing prison. The youngest of these men was Joe Diamond, just nineteen years old. While he sat in the Raymond Street jail, awaiting to be transferred to the death house in Sing Sing, he wrote several poems on the wall of his cell. One poem was: Maybe it's because I remember just about two years ago; When we stood all full of sorrow, in a house so full of woe. It was the next day after Father's soul had gone to rest, When I promised faithful before God, I'd do my best.

Evidently, two years before, when his father passed away it caused him to think and he promised himself he would live a better life. Brother, Sister, it takes something more than trying. It takes something more than turning over a new leaf. It takes CHRIST! It takes the blood of Jesus to change and transform your life. No. Two years later Joe Diamond found himself in the death house at the end of a life of sin. But oh, my friend, death is not the end. My Bible says, "After death, the Judgment." Another poem Joe wrote on the wall of his cell was:

Tonight as I sit and ponder,
Alone in my own grim cell
It strikes me hard, and I wonder,
Can it be lonelier in hell?

Yes, Hell is a place of loneliness. You will have plenty of company there. But hear what I say: Everyone will be so taken up with his or her own suffering, torment, memory, and remorse that they will have no time for anyone else and you will feel you are all alone. Yes, Hell is a place of loneliness.

235

Again I say, *Hell is a place where desires cannot be satisfied.* Every passion, every desire you have will be multiplied a hundred percent in Hell. In this life, when you want to smoke, you can satisfy that desire. The rich man could have anything he wanted to drink, but in Hell he asked for a plainer beverage: water; and couldn't even get one drop. Ah yes, desire cannot be satisfied in Hell. Let me tell you my friend, there will be no modern conveniences in Hell, and they will not serve you any booze on a tray. The burning torments of your desires will sear your soul, but you will not be able to satisfy those desires.

I cannot tell you how horrible Hell is, but my Bible says, "There shall be weeping, and wailing and gnashing of teeth."

Hell is a place without hope! When it's a rainy day, Mother always says, "Never mind, honey, the sun will shine tomorrow." Yes, no matter how dark and dreary the day, we can always anticipate a brighter tomorrow. Not so in Hell. Hell is a place without hope. If a man is sent to prison, he always has the hope of being pardoned for good behavior. Let me tell you my friend, if you spurn my Jesus, if you refuse to obey God, there is no second chance after death. *Hell is a place without hope.*

Yes, Hell is the *Penitentiary of the Damned!* Did you hear me, I said, *Hell is a world without hope.* Hell is forever and forever. See those demons of Satan as they dance around lost souls in impish delight, singing one word, one horrible note, "You're chained here, forever, forever, forever!"

Ah Christians, I wish I could arouse you so that you would realize that the souls you fail to testify to about Jesus may be lost forever, forever. My esteemed coworker, Brother Vander Jagt, never lets a person pass him without dealing with him about his soul. Why? Because he knows Hell is forever. In Revelations, the 14th chapter, my Bible tells us *Hell is forever.* "The smoke of their torment ascendeth up forever and ever and there is no rest day or night."

No rest day or night. Think of it. No rest in Hell! When you are tired, how good a bed feels, but there will be no rest in Hell. Yes in Hell you will be beyond God forever, beyond the Bible forever, and beyond the Saviour forever. Listen to me, I want you to get this. You either take the blood or the blame. Did you hear me? You either take the blood or the blame. Yes, you either take the cross or the curse. You either take Jesus as your Saviour or be banished from the presence of God forever and ever.

Praise God, there is a way of escape; there is hope for you. The blood of Jesus Christ cleanseth us from all sin. Just believe in the Lord Jesus Christ and thou shalt be saved. John 3:16— "For God so loved the world that He gave His only begotten Son that whosoever believeth in Him should not perish but have everlasting life." You can be wicked if you want to Mister. You can go on in your own way, but I have warned you. "The wicked shall be turned into Hell and all the nations that forget God." "It is appointed unto man once to die and after death, the judgment." Judgment is coming fast. Death is on the track of every man, woman, boy, and girl. When God's atomic judgment descends on this doomed world, there isn't a human hand that can stop it. Come to my Jesus—the ark of safety.

237

The door of mercy is still open. Tomorrow may be forever too late for you. [At this point, Marjoe dramatically sang "The Great Judgment Morning."]

I may be only six years old, but I know what it is for a soul to be lost. If I could carry you to Jesus, I would do it. When Jesus called me to preach, all He commissioned me to do was "Preach the Word." Friend, I've done my best tonight. Christians, you do your best by bringing someone to Jesus now. Sinner, hasten, don't wait, don't procrastinate, move fast! Come to Jesus now, I plead with you.

73 74 75 76 77 10 9 8 7 6 5 4 3 2 1